LIBERTY & JUSTICE
for all

by Vicki Lynn Oehlke

Landauer Books

Liberty & Justice
for all

Projects, Photos, Illustrations and Text Copyright© 2007 Vicki Lynn Oehlke

Book Copyright© 2008 by Landauer Books
A division of Landauer Corporation
3100 101st Street
Urbandale, Iowa 50322
800/557-2144   www.landauercorp.com

For Landauer Corporation
President/Publisher: Jeramy Lanigan Landauer
Director of Sales & Operations: Kitty Jacobson
Art Director: Laurel Albright
Contributing Art Director: Linda Bender
Managing Editor: Jeri Simon
Contributing Technical Editor: Kimber von Heukelem

For the author Vicki Lynn Oehlke
Photographer: Arika Johnson
Graphic Artist: Laura Scott
Piecing and Pattern Testing: Sherry Beckstrand, Betty Jo Erickson,
Joyce Hammer, Kim Kenner
Long Arm Machine Quilter: Barb Simons

ISBN 13: 978-0-9793711-8-9
ISBN 10: 0-9793711-8-x

This book printed on acid-free paper.
Printed in China

10 9 8 7 6 5 4 3 1
Liberty & Justice for all by Vicki Lynn Oehlke
Library of Congress Control Number: 2008920306

LIBERTY & JUSTICE
for all

Table of Contents

Went to make an
Army quilt on Army green
wool. 2020.

3

4

LIBERTY & JUSTICE for all

began with the quilt made for my son, Jeb, upon graduation from UND Law School. Jeb had spent a summer taking law classes in Oslo, Norway, and had the opportunity to visit several other countries as well.

Not asking for much, he only wanted a quilt for his queen-size bed with all the flags of all the countries he had visited and "Lady Justice" standing in the middle holding the "Scales of Justice." Scales I could do. The Lady was a bit too complicated for me.

My husband, Dave, helped in the designing of Jeb's quilt, and he has helped me again this evening as I struggled with the question, "Should I change this to an iron-on appliqué pattern?" I was questioning the decision I had made, time and time again, whenever a new quilt was sewn for this book. Why? The amount of fabric required to sew the emblems with two layers of fabric, my preferred method of appliqué. I love the dimension, richness, feel, look, and the ease of construction this method gives me.

My husband's comment? "I would think anyone making a quilt from this book is going to want to do the absolute best job they can. If that means buying a couple extra yards of fabric, I really don't think it will matter to them."

Thank you, Honey! You are right.

And thank you to all of you who have purchased this book to sew one of these patriotic quilts for yourself or someone you love. It is my hope you will enjoy my method of appliqué, and even more so, the final product.

The most important thank you is to all our Service Men and Women, past and present. You do go above and beyond. I dedicate this book to all of you. THANK YOU!

Vicki Lynn

5

SEAM ALLOWANCE
Stitch a $1/4$" seam unless otherwise stated.

PRESSING *SEAMS*
Press to one side unless otherwise noted.

Pressing directions are given in the instructions for seams that need to be pressed a certain direction for ease of construction.

Sewing Emblems: **General Instructions**

note: Find the emblem templates in the back of your book.

Prepare Appliqué:

- **Trace** emblem piece to paper side (dull side) of freezer paper.

- **Lay** fabrics cut for each emblem section with **right sides together.**
- **Press** and **pin** each traced section onto corresponding fabric.

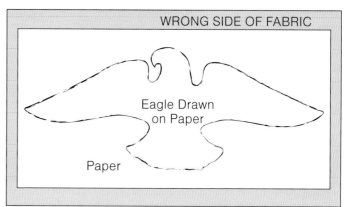

- **Sew** on the line **leaving raw edges open** where indicated.
- **Remove paper.**
- **Trim excess** fabric leaving $1/8$" to $1/4$" seam allowance.
- **Clip** curves and points.

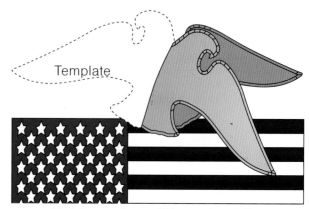

Emblem – Sewn, Trimmed and Clipped

Turning Your Sewn Appliqué Pieces:
With wrong sides of fabric still out:
- **Place** sewn emblem on top of the template.
- Make sure emblem is facing correct direction.
- **Cut** a slit in top layer of fabric.
- **Turn** and **press.**

Stitch or **press** on any small appliqué pieces indicated for your emblem.

Small Appliqué Pieces

Preparing Bias:

Cut enough strips to equal the length you need.

Cut

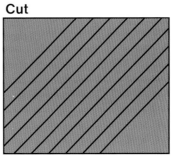

45° Angle

Sew strips together **end to end** to obtain length needed.

Stitch

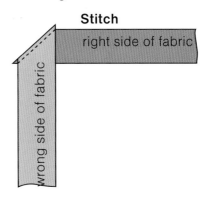

right side of fabric

wrong side of fabric

Press seams in bias **open** instead of to one side.

Press Strip Open

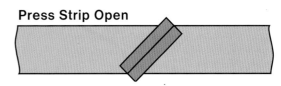

Fold strips in half, right side of fabric showing. **Stitch with** ¹/₄" **seam allowance.**

Fold and Stitch

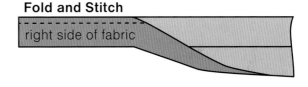

right side of fabric

Press, positioning seam in **center of back.**

Press seam allowance to one side.

Trim to approximately ¹/₈".

Your bias is ready.

Various Stitches
That could be used around the stars.

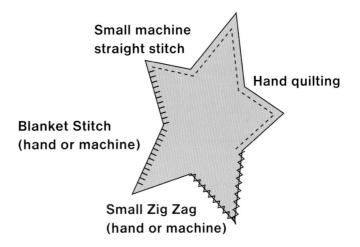

Small machine straight stitch

Hand quilting

Blanket Stitch (hand or machine)

Small Zig Zag (hand or machine)

Liberty

yardage

Fabric requirements

Lap/Wall Size 50" x 52"

Flag & Background Star

Colors	Yardage
A – Blue	fat quarter
B – Red	1/4 yard
C – White	1/3 yard
D – Background (includes outer border)	3 yards
E – Large Star (Tan)	1 1/4 yards
F – Inner Border	1 1/3 yards

Emblem

G – Gold	1 yard
I – Brown	fat quarter

Binding & Backing

Binding	1/2 yard
Backing	3 1/4 yards

cutting

Cut in order

Flag

	Size	Use
A – Blue	1 – 7 1/2" x 9"	Star Background
B – Red - first cut	3 strips 1 1/2" x 43"	Flag Stripes
from these cut	4 – 1 1/2" x 13"	Flag Stripes
	3 – 1 1/2" x 21 1/2"	Flag Stripes
C – White - first cut	3 strips 1 1/2" x 43"	Flag Stripes
from these cut	3 – 1 1/2" x 13"	Flag Stripes
	3 – 1 1/2" x 21 1/2"	Flag Stripes

Background Star

	Size	Use
D – Background	2 – 10 1/8" x 16 5/8"	Unit 1
	2 – 9 5/8" x 8 1/8"	Unit 2
	2 – 11 1/8" x 9 1/4"	Unit 3
	2 – 6 1/8" x 14 1/8"	Unit 3C
E – Large Star (Tan)	1 – 10 1/8" x 11 1/8"	Unit 1
	1 – 1 1/2" x 37"	Unit 1 Bottom
	2 – 10 5/8" x 8 1/8"	Unit 2
	1 – 11 1/8" x 26 3/4"	Unit 3

Inner Border

Option 1 shown here. See page 121 for yardage and cutting instructions for both options.

Outer Border (OB)

	Size	Use
D – Background	lengthwise cut	
	2 – 5" x 54"	OB Top & Bottom
	2 – 5" x 43"	OB Sides
E – Large Star (Tan)	2 – 5" x 7"	Top Star Point #1
	4 – 4" x 5"	Side Star Points #2 & #3
	4 – 6" x 7"	Bottom Star Points #4 & #5

Stars

	Star Type	Amounts
C – White	Pieced	1 – 1 1/2" x 12"
G – Gold	Pieced	1 – 1 1/2" x 12"
Solid Stars	Use remaining white and gold fabrics	

Instructions given are for a Lap/Wall size quilt. If you wish to make a Queen size quilt, contact the author, Vicki Lynn Oehlke.
Phone: 701-662-6795
or email:
willowberry@gondtc.com

Liberty

Constructing the Flag

The first step in creating your quilt is to construct the flag. This section will take you step-by-step through the process for the Liberty quilt.

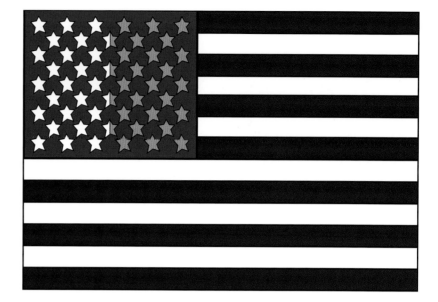

Appliquéing the Stars

Trace 50 stars on paper side of fusible web.

Press stars to **wrong side** of fabric before cutting them out.

Refer to the "Stars Needed" chart, next page, to find the number of star types for the Liberty emblem.

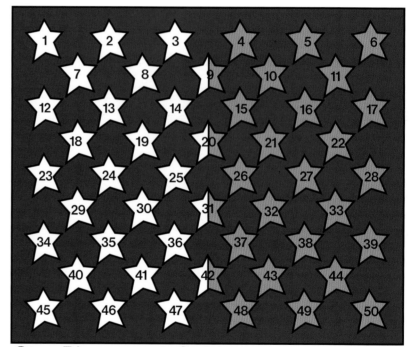

Star Placement Guide

For accurate star placement, refer to the full-size template found at the back of the book.

Stars Needed

White 23	Gold 23	Pieced 4

Templates for solid and pieced stars are reversed for cutting

Preparing Pieced Stars:

Placing right sides together, **sew** the **pieced star strips**, **lengthwise** as shown, using a 1/4" seam allowance.

double pieced star strip

Right Side Up

Press seams open and **trim** seams to 1/8" or less.

Trim Seam Allowance

Refer to "Stars Needed" chart, above, and press the number of stars needed to wrong side of fabric. **Align seams** with lines on star templates.

Cut stars out on line.

Sample of Pieced Star Strips

Follow star placement guides to arrange your stars on the blue star background.

Press stars in place.
Stitch around stars by hand or machine. See various stitches on page 7 for stitching ideas.

Piecing the Flag

note: Use a slightly longer stitch than usual as you will be ripping out large portions of these seams later. Use a regular stitch length if you don't plan to add one of the emblems.

Sew the 4 shorter red strips and 3 shorter white strips together as in diagram.

Press seams toward Red.

Sew the red & white unit to the right side of the blue background with appliquéd stars.

Press seam toward Blue.

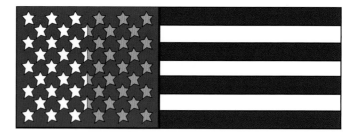

Sew the 3 longer white strips and the 3 longer red strips together as in diagram.

Press seams toward Red.

Sew this unit to the bottom of the stars and stripes unit.

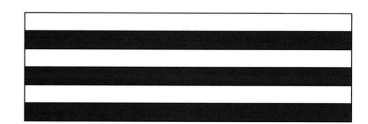

Press seam toward Red/Blue.

Flag measures:
Lap/Wall: 13 1/2" x 21 1/2"

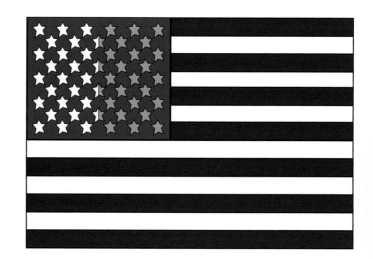

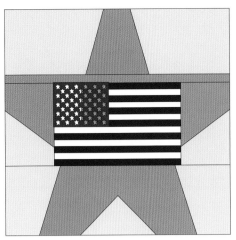

Constructing the Large Background Star

The second step in creating your quilt is to construct the large background star. This section will take you step-by-step through the process for the Liberty quilt.

Step 1: Preparing Background and Large Star Pieces
Measure, mark and cut from **mark to corner** as shown in diagrams with a **dotted line**.

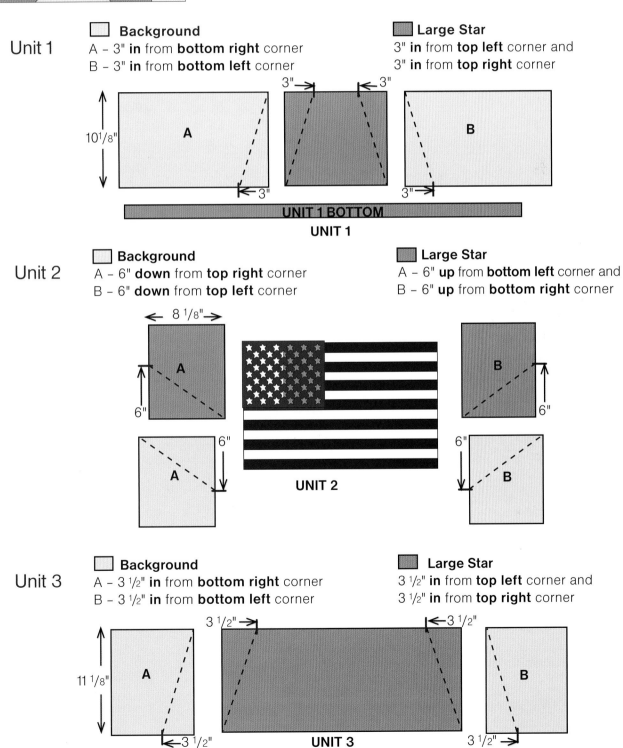

Unit 1

☐ **Background**
A – 3" in from **bottom right** corner
B – 3" in from **bottom left** corner

☐ **Large Star**
3" in from **top left** corner and
3" in from **top right** corner

Unit 2

☐ **Background**
A – 6" **down** from **top right** corner
B – 6" **down** from **top left** corner

☐ **Large Star**
A – 6" **up** from **bottom left** corner and
B – 6" **up** from **bottom right** corner

Unit 3

☐ **Background**
A – 3 1/2" **in** from **bottom right** corner
B – 3 1/2" **in** from **bottom left** corner

☐ **Large Star**
3 1/2" **in** from **top left** corner and
3 1/2" **in** from **top right** corner

Step 2: Pinning And Sewing

Pin And Sew Unit 1

Join Unit 1A background to **left side** of **Unit 1** large star.

Join Unit 1B background to **right side** of **Unit 1** large star.

Sew Unit 1 bottom large star tan to **bottom** of the **above joined units**.

Press toward **gold strip**.

UNIT 1

Pin And Sew Unit 2

Join Unit 2A background to **Unit 2A** large star.

Join Unit 2B background to **Unit 2B** large star.

Sew Unit 2A to the **left side** of your **flag**.

Sew Unit 2B to the **right side** of your **flag**.

Press toward large star.

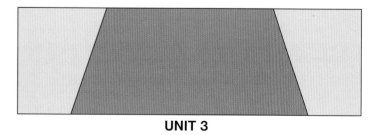

UNIT 2

Pin And Sew Unit 3

Join Unit 3A background to the **left side** of **Unit 3** large star.

Join Unit 3B background to the **right side** of **Unit 3** large star.

Press toward large star.

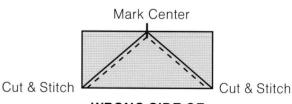

UNIT 3

Appliqué Unit 3C

Lay Unit 3C background star pieces **right sides together**.

Mark center of the 14 1/8" top edge.

Cut triangle
- Line up ruler from center mark to bottom right corner. Cut.
- Line up ruler from center mark to bottom left corner. Cut.

Mark Center

Cut & Stitch   Cut & Stitch

WRONG SIDE OF FABRIC

UNIT 3C

Prepare for appliqué
- Sew the two sides just cut.
- Trim top point.
- Turn right side out.
- Press.

Center appliqué
- Press pieced Unit 3 in half by lining up the two seams.
- Lay Unit 3 flat, right side up.
- Line up raw edge of triangle with the bottom edge of pieced Unit 3, and the point of the triangle with the pressed crease.
- Pin and stitch triangle to large star fabric by hand or machine.

Trim out the two layers of excess fabric from the back if you wish.

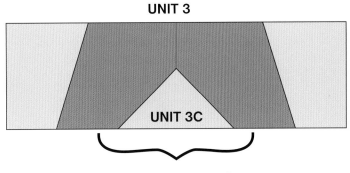

UNIT 3

UNIT 3C

Center & Appliqué

Step 3: Joining Units

Line up the **center of the top star point** (Unit 1 – bottom edge) with the **center of the flag** (Unit 2 – top edge).

Lay flat and **pin seam** from center out.

Stitch Unit 1 to **Unit 2**.

Press seam toward the **flag**.

Line up the **flag center** (bottom edge) with the **center crease of Unit 3**.

Lay flat and **pin seam** from center out.

Stitch and **press** toward **flag**.

Trim finished quilt center if necessary.

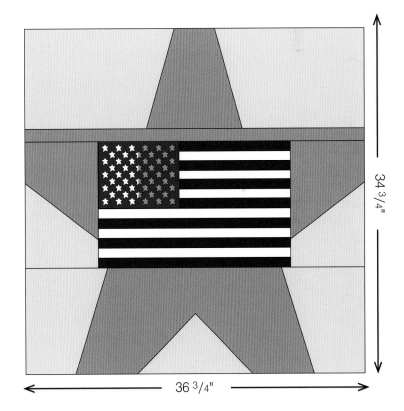

34 3/4"

36 3/4"

Liberty

Adding an Emblem

The third step in creating your quilt is to add an emblem. This section will take you step-by-step through the process for the Liberty quilt.

note: Find the emblem templates in the back of your book.

Sewing the Emblem

Prepare Appliqué:

note: Trace the emblem from the templates located in the back of your book.

See General Instructions on page 6 for detailed description of how to prepare the appliqué.

Using the template found in the back of the book, **trace** emblem piece to paper side (dull side) of freezer paper. **Lay** fabrics cut for each emblem section with **right sides together. Press** and **pin** each traced section onto corresponding fabric. **Sew** on the line **leaving raw edges open** where indicated. **Remove paper. Trim excess** fabric leaving 1/8" to 1/4" seam allowance. **Clip** curves and points.

Turning Your Sewn Appliqué Pieces:

With wrong sides of fabric still out, **place** sewn emblem on top of the template. Make sure emblem is facing correct direction. **Cut** a slit in top layer of fabric. **Turn** and **press.**

Stitch or **press** on any small appliqué pieces indicated for your emblem.
Refer to the template for placement of any small appliqué pieces needed on your emblem and for placement in the flag.

Small appliqué pieces on Bell Top A:
Prepare these with 2 layers of fabric as you did the large bell pieces.

Appliqué into position by hand or straight stitch on machine.

Crack on Bell:
Option #1

Bias appliqué using a brown fabric:
Cut bias 1 1/4" wide. You will need 12". See General Instructions on page 7 to make a bias strip.

Option #2

Embroider with brown thread: This can be done by machine or hand. Crack should be approximately 3/8" wide.

Possible Stitches below– BE CREATIVE – the possibilities are endless!

Option #3

Machine quilt the crack onto the bell. The crack should only show on the bell, NOT on the flag stripes.
With any of the above options, use the Liberty Bell template for placement of the crack.

Small Appliqué Pieces

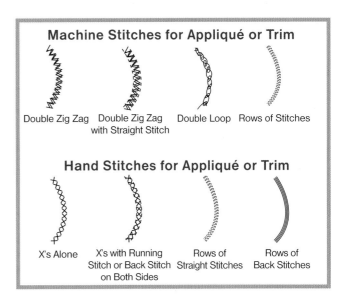

Machine Stitches for Appliqué or Trim

Double Zig Zag   Double Zig Zag with Straight Stitch   Double Loop   Rows of Stitches

Hand Stitches for Appliqué or Trim

X's Alone   X's with Running Stitch or Back Stitch on Both Sides   Rows of Straight Stitches   Rows of Back Stitches

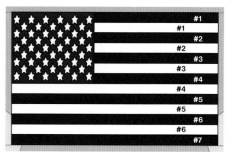

Numbered Stripes Chart

Weaving the Emblem

Position emblem piece(s) on the flag.

Follow emblem templates to center and position emblem piece(s).

Place a small gold safety pin in each seam of the flag where seam and emblem meet.

Pin emblem piece(s) in place leaving any part of the emblem below #6 red stripe loose.

Weave lower part of flag.

You will be weaving the emblem under the red stripe and over the white stripe.

Open top seam of red strip #7 between gold pins.

open seam

Pull lower portion of emblem piece through seam to the back of the quilt center.

Lay quilt out flat so seam lies in place.

Pin seam.

Using matching red thread, sew seam closed with straight stitch close to edge of red stripe.

Open bottom seam of flag between gold pins.

Bring bottom of emblem UP through seam.

Sew seam closed as before.

Weaving the Emblem

Remove straight pins.

Fold upper part of emblem down and open bottom seam of red stripe #6 between gold pins.

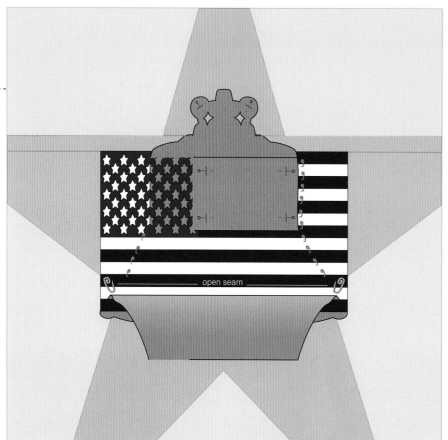

Pull emblem UP through seam to back of flag.

Pin rest of emblem up to keep out of seam as you straight stitch seam closed as before.

Continue weaving the emblem into the lower portion of flag until emblem is brought up to the back of flag in the seam along the bottom of the blue star background and bottom of red stripe #4.

Use matching thread on both the blue and red fabrics as you straight stitch seam closed.

Weave under blue background of stars and upper stripes.

Open top seam of red stripe #4 between gold pins.

Open the seam of white strip #3 and blue background of stars.

Bring raw edge of emblem DOWN through seam to BACK of flag.

Weaving the Emblem

Emblems that weave under blue background:
Fold and pin emblem as shown in picture to keep emblem and stripes flat as you pin in place and sew along edge of red stripe with matching thread.

Leave seam of blue background and white stripe #3 open. We will sew this after emblem weaving is finished.

Open bottom seam of red stripe #3.

Bring emblem through to back. Topstitch seam closed as before.

Continue weaving in this manner until emblem is brought through the bottom seam of red stripe #1. Topstitch.

Open top seam of flag between gold pins.

Bring raw edge of emblem top DOWN through seam to BACK of quilt.

Topstitch seam closed using matching blue and matching red thread.

Topstitch with matching blue thread along right side of blue background for stars to close the open seams.

Continue topstitching around blue background to make it uniform if you wish.

Finish edges of emblem.

Pin emblem edges to flag and background at open edges.

Topstitch emblem to quilt center using a stitch of your choice. See various stitches on page 7 for stitching ideas.

The last step in creating your quilt is adding the borders. See page 120 for detailed instructions for adding borders to finish your quilt.

Justice yardage

Fabric requirements

Use these fabric requirements for the Basic quilt pictured on page 120. Eliminate yardage for the emblem.

Use these fabric requirements for the Basic quilt pictured on page120.

Lap/Wall Size   50" x 52"

Flag & Background Star

Colors	Yardage
A – Blue	fat quarter
B – Red	1/4 yard
C – White	1/3 yard
D – Background (includes outer border)	3 yards
E – Large Star (Tan)	1 1/4 yards
F – Inner Border	1 1/3 yards

Emblem

G – Gold	1/3 yard

Binding & Backing

Binding	1/2 yard
Backing	3 1/4 yards

cutting

Cut in order

Flag

	Size	Use
A – Blue	1 – 7 1/2" x 9"	Star Background
B – Red - first cut	3 strips 1 1/2" x 43"	Flag Stripes
from these cut	4 – 1 1/2" x 13"	Flag Stripes
	3 – 1 1/2" x 21 1/2"	Flag Stripes
C – White - first cut	3 strips 1 1/2" x 43"	Flag Stripes
from these cut	3 – 1 1/2" x 13"	Flag Stripes
	3 – 1 1/2" x 21 1/2"	Flag Stripes

Background Star

	Size	Use
D – Background	2 – 10 1/8" x 16 5/8"	Unit 1
	2 – 9 5/8" x 8 1/8"	Unit 2
	2 – 11 1/8" x 9 1/4"	Unit 3
	2 – 6 1/8" x 14 1/8"	Unit 3C
E – Large Star (Tan)	1 – 10 1/8" x 11 1/8"	Unit 1
	1 – 1 1/2" x 37"	Unit 1 Bottom
	2 – 10 5/8" x 8 1/8"	Unit 2
	1 – 11 1/8" x 26 3/4"	Unit 3

Inner Border

See page 121 for border options.

Outer Border (OB)

	Size	Use
D – Background	lengthwise cut	
	2 – 5" x 54"	OB Top & Bottom
	2 – 5" x 43"	OB Sides
E – Large Star (Tan)	2 – 5" x 7"	Top Star Point #1
	4 – 4" x 5"	Side Star Points #2 & #3
	4 – 6" x 7"	Bottom Star Points #4 & #5

Stars

	Star Type	Amounts
D – White	All Solid Stars	Use remaining white fabric

Emblem

	Size	Use
G – Gold	2 – 4 1/2" x 16 1/2"	Scale Base
	1 – 1 3/4" x 14 1/2"	Scale Arm
	4 – 1 1/2" x 4 1/2"	Scale Pans

Instructions given are for a Lap/Wall size quilt. If you wish to make a Queen size quilt, contact the author, Vicki Lynn Oehlke. Phone: 701-662-6795 or email: willowberry@gondtc.com

Justice

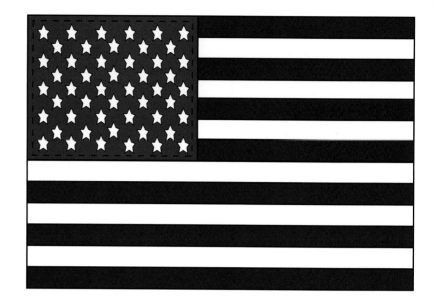

Constructing the Flag

The first step in creating your quilt is to construct the flag. This section will take you step-by-step through the process for the Justice quilt.

Appliquéing the Stars

Trace 50 stars on paper side of fusible web.

Press stars to **wrong side** of fabric before cutting them out.

Refer to the "Stars Needed" chart, below, to find the number of star types for the Justice emblem.

Star Placement Guide
For accurate star placement, refer to the full-size template found at the back of the book.

Stars Needed

**White
50**

Template for stars has been reversed for cutting

Piecing the Flag

note: Use a slightly longer stitch than usual as you will be ripping out large portions of these seams later. Use a regular stitch length if you don't plan to add one of the emblems.

Sew the 4 shorter red strips and 3 shorter white strips together as in diagram.

Press seams toward Red.

Sew the red & white unit to the right side of the blue background with appliquéd stars.

Press seam toward Blue.

Sew the 3 longer white strips and the 3 longer red strips together as in diagram.

Press seams toward Red.

Sew this unit to the bottom of the stars and stripes unit.

Press seam toward Red/Blue.

Flag measures:
Lap/Wall: 13 1/2" x 21 1/2"

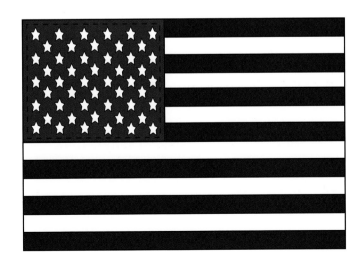

Constructing the Large Background Star

The second step in creating your quilt is to construct the large background star. This section will take you step-by-step through the process for the Justice quilt.

Step 1: Preparing Background and Large Star Pieces

Measure, **mark and cut** from **mark to corner** as shown in diagrams with a **dotted line**.

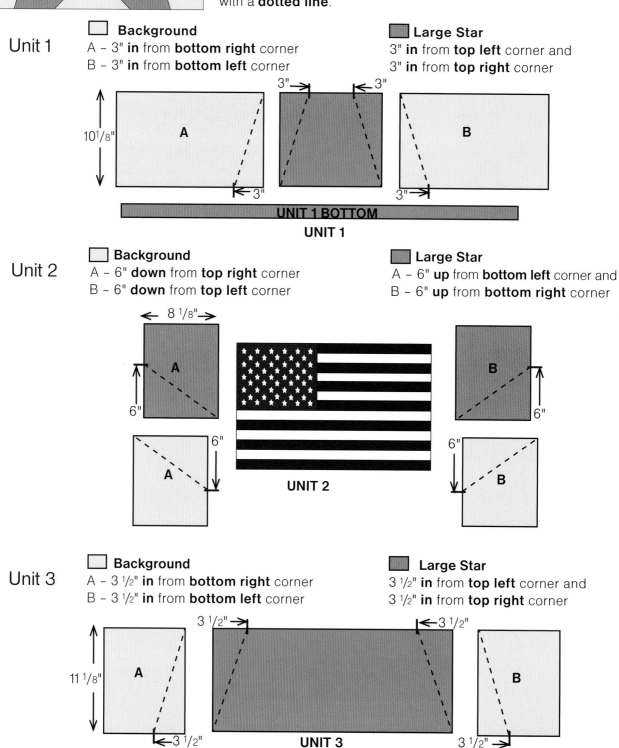

Unit 1

☐ **Background**
A – 3" in from **bottom right** corner
B – 3" **in** from **bottom left** corner

▨ **Large Star**
3" **in** from **top left** corner and
3" **in** from **top right** corner

10 1/8"

3"   3"

A

B

3"   3"

UNIT 1 BOTTOM

UNIT 1

Unit 2

☐ **Background**
A – 6" **down** from **top right** corner
B – 6" **down** from **top left** corner

▨ **Large Star**
A – 6" **up** from **bottom left** corner and
B – 6" **up** from **bottom right** corner

← 8 1/8" →

A

6"

A   6"

B

6"

6"   B

UNIT 2

Unit 3

☐ **Background**
A – 3 1/2" **in** from **bottom right** corner
B – 3 1/2" **in** from **bottom left** corner

▨ **Large Star**
3 1/2" **in** from **top left** corner and
3 1/2" **in** from **top right** corner

3 1/2"   ←3 1/2"

11 1/8"   A

B

←3 1/2"   3 1/2"

UNIT 3

Step 2: Pinning And Sewing

Pin And Sew Unit 1

Join Unit 1A background to **left side** of **Unit 1** large star.

Join Unit 1B background to **right side** of **Unit 1** large star.

Sew Unit 1 bottom large star tan to **bottom** of the **above joined units**.

Press toward **tan strip**.

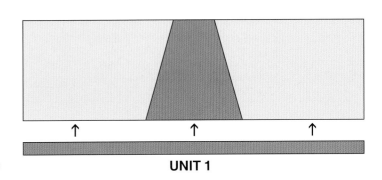

UNIT 1

Pin And Sew Unit 2

Join Unit 2A background to **Unit 2A** large star.

Join Unit 2B background to **Unit 2B** large star.

Sew Unit 2A to the **left side** of your **flag**.

Sew Unit 2B to the **right side** of your **flag**.

Press toward large star.

UNIT 2

Pin And Sew Unit 3

Join Unit 3A background to the **left side** of **Unit 3** large star.

Join Unit 3B background to the **right side** of **Unit 3** large star.

Press toward large star.

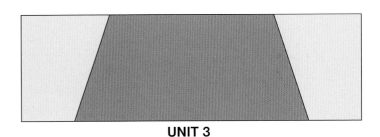

UNIT 3

Appliqué Unit 3C

Lay Unit 3C background star pieces **right sides together**.

Mark center of the 14 1/8" top edge.

Cut triangle
- Line up ruler from center mark to bottom right corner. Cut.
- Line up ruler from center mark to bottom left corner. Cut.

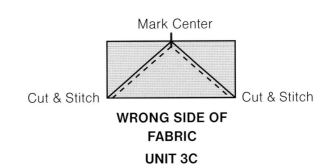

Mark Center

Cut & Stitch   Cut & Stitch

WRONG SIDE OF FABRIC

UNIT 3C

Prepare for appliqué
- Sew the two sides just cut.
- Trim top point.
- Turn right side out.
- Press.

Center appliqué
- Press pieced Unit 3 in half by lining up the two seams.
- Lay Unit 3 flat, right side up.
- Line up raw edge of triangle with the bottom edge of pieced Unit 3, and the **point** of the triangle with the pressed **crease**.
- Pin and stitch triangle to large star fabric by hand or machine.

Trim out the two layers of excess fabric from the back if you wish.

Joining Units

Line up the **center of the top star point** (Unit 1 – bottom edge) with the **center of the flag** (Unit 2 – top edge).

Lay flat and **pin seam** from center out.

Stitch Unit 1 to **Unit 2**.

Press seam toward the **flag**.

Line up the **flag center** (bottom edge) with the **center crease of Unit 3**.

Lay flat and **pin seam** from center out.

Stitch and **press** toward **flag**.

Trim finished quilt center if necessary.

UNIT 3

UNIT 3C

Center & Appliqué

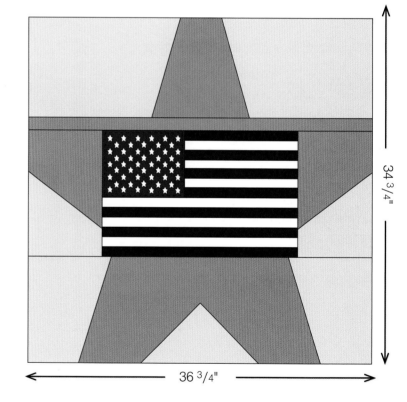

34 3/4"

36 3/4"

Justice
Adding an Emblem

The third step in creating your quilt is to add an emblem. This section will take you step-by-step through the process for the Justice quilt.

Sewing the Emblem

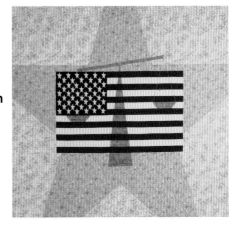

Prepare Appliqué:

note: Prepare the Justice emblem by following the piecing instructions below.

See General Instructions on page 6 for detailed description of how to prepare the appliqué.

Right sides of fabric together.
Base

BASE

Mark Center

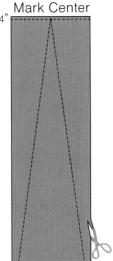

Mark or **stitch** 1/4" down from top edge of fabric.

Mark center on the 1/4" line.

Mark 1/4" in from each bottom corner.

Draw straight lines from **center mark to bottom corner marks**.

Stitch on these lines.

Stitch 1/4" up from bottom edge.

Trim excess fabric from sides. **Turn** as covered in the General Instructions for "Sewing Emblems."

Arm

ARMS

Fold in **half lengthwise, right sides together**.

Sew ends.

Turn right side out.

Stitch long seam.

Press seam **to back**, including stitching.

Pans

PANS

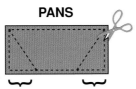

Stitch around outside edge with 1/4" seam allowance.

Mark in from each bottom corner on stitched line 1".

1"   1"

Stitch from top corner of stitching to mark on bottom seam as shown in Pans diagram.

Trim sides and points – **turn** as directed in the General Instructions for "Sewing Emblems."

Chains from Arm Ends to Pans

After scale pieces have been appliquéd to quilt, **mark** straight lines from bottom corner of arm to the two top corners of the pan.

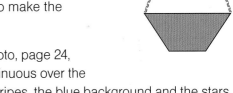

Stitch (by machine or hand) a decorative stitch in gold thread on these lines to make the chains.

As shown in photo, page 24, stitching is continuous over the red and white stripes, the blue background and the stars.

Another option:
The chains could be machine quilted into the quilt.

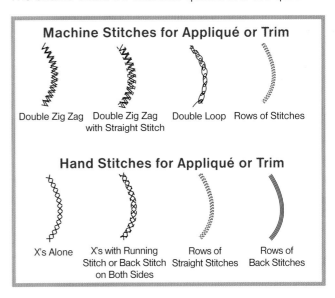

Machine Stitches for Appliqué or Trim

Double Zig Zag | Double Zig Zag with Straight Stitch | Double Loop | Rows of Stitches

Hand Stitches for Appliqué or Trim

X's Alone | X's with Running Stitch or Back Stitch on Both Sides | Rows of Straight Stitches | Rows of Back Stitches

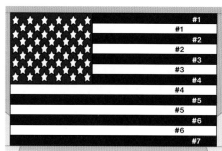

Numbered Stripes Chart

Weaving the Emblem

Position emblem piece(s) on the flag.

Follow emblem templates to center and position emblem piece(s).

Place a small gold safety pin in each seam of the flag where seam and emblem meet.

Pin emblem piece(s) in place leaving any part of the emblem below #6 red stripe loose.

Weave lower part of flag.
You will be weaving the emblem under the red stripe and over the white stripe.

Open top seam of red strip #7 between gold pins.

NOTE: Scale pans and arm are not woven. Appliqué onto flag as shown in template.

Pull lower portion of emblem piece through seam to the back of the quilt center.

Lay quilt out flat so seam lies in place.

Pin seam.

Using matching red thread, sew seam closed with straight stitch close to edge of red stripe.

Open bottom seam of flag between gold pins.

Bring bottom of emblem UP through seam.

Sew seam closed as before.

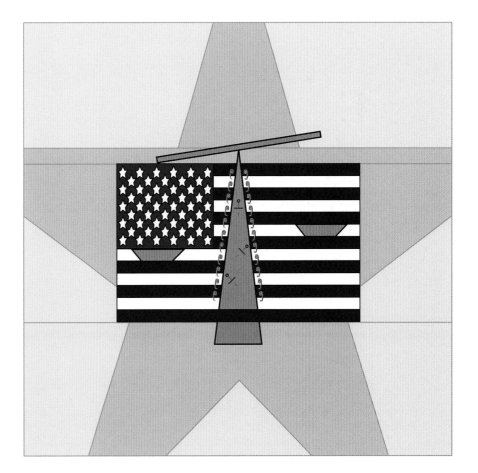

Weaving the Emblem

Remove straight pins.

Fold upper part of emblem down and open bottom seam of red stripe #6 between gold pins.

Pull emblem UP through seam to back of flag.

Pin rest of emblem up to keep out of seam as you straight stitch seam closed as before.

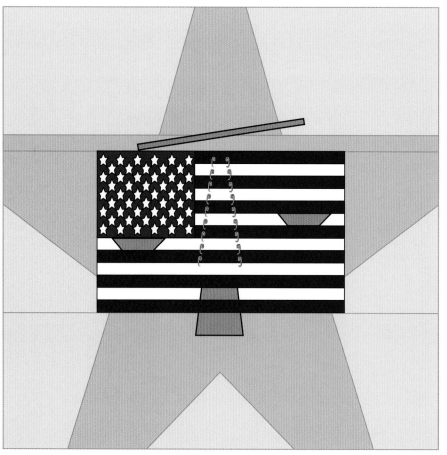

Continue weaving the emblem into the lower portion of flag until emblem is brought up to the back of flag in the seam along the bottom of the blue star background and bottom of red stripe #4.

Use matching red thread as you straight stitch seam closed.

Weave the emblem into upper stripes.

Open top seam of red stripe #4 between gold pins.

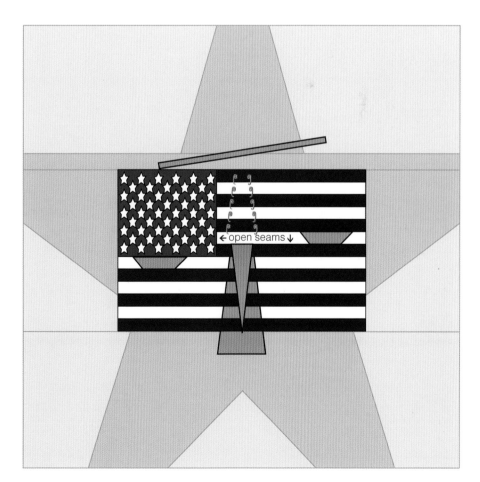

Weaving the Emblem

Bring emblem UP through seam to front of flag.

Open bottom seam of red stripe #3.

Bring emblem through to back. Topstitch seam closed as before.

Continue weaving in this manner until emblem is brought through the bottom seam of red stripe #1. Topstitch.

Open top seam of flag between gold pins.

Bring emblem UP through seam to front of quilt.

Topstitch seams closed using matching red thread.

Finish edges of emblem.

Pin emblem edges to flag and background at open edges.

Topstitch emblem to quilt center using a stitch of your choice. See various stitches on page 7 for stitching ideas.

The last step in creating your quilt is adding the borders. See page 120 for detailed instructions for adding borders to finish your quilt.

Army yardage

Fabric requirements

Lap/Wall Size 50" x 52"

Flag & Background Star

Colors	**Yardage**
A – Blue	fat quarter
B – Red	1/4 yard
C – White	1/3 yard
D – Background (includes outer border)	3 yards
E – Large Star (Tan)	1 1/4 yards
F – Inner Border – Black	1 1/2 yards
Gold	1/3 yard

Emblem

Colors	**Yardage**
G – Gold	1/2 yard
C – White	Fat Quarters (fq) & Scraps
H – Black	2/3 yard

Binding & Backing

Binding	1/2 yard
Backing	3 1/4 yards

cutting

Cut in order

This quilt I'd like to do in honor of My Dad. He was a veteran of the Korean War. Very Active Vet. [illegible]

Flag

	Size	**Use**
A – Blue	1 – 7 1/2" x 9"	Star Background
B – Red - first cut	3 strips 1 1/2" x 43"	Flag Stripes
from these cut	4 – 1 1/2" x 13"	Flag Stripes
	3 – 1 1/2" x 21 1/2"	Flag Stripes
C – White - first cut	3 strips 1 1/2" x 43"	Flag Stripes
from these cut	3 – 1 1/2" x 13"	Flag Stripes
	3 – 1 1/2" x 21 1/2"	Flag Stripes

Background Star

D – Background	2 – 10 1/8" x 16 5/8"	Unit 1
	2 – 9 5/8" x 8 1/8"	Unit 2
	2 – 11 1/8" x 9 1/4"	Unit 3
	2 – 6 1/8" x 14 1/8"	Unit 3C
E – Large Star (Tan)	1 – 10 1/8" x 11 1/8"	Unit 1
	1 – 1 1/2" x 37"	Unit 1 Bottom
	2 – 10 5/8" x 8 1/8"	Unit 2
	1 – 11 1/8" x 26 3/4"	Unit 3

Inner Border

Option 2 shown here. See page 121 for yardage and cutting instructions for both options.

Outer Border (OB)

D – Background	lengthwise cut	
	2 – 5" x 54"	OB Top & Bottom
	2 – 5" x 43"	OB Sides
E – Large Star (Tan)	2 – 5" x 7"	Top Star Point #1
	4 – 4" x 5"	Side Star Points #2 & #3
	4 – 6" x 7"	Bottom Star Points #4 & #5

Stars

	Star Type	
C – White	triple	1 – 3/4" x 2"
	pieced with black	1 – 1 1/2" x 6"
F – Black	triple	1 – 7/8" x 2"
	pieced with gold	1 – 1 1/2" x 23"
	pieced with white	1 – 1 1/2" x 6"
G – Gold	triple	1 – 3/4" x 2"
	pieced with black	1 – 1 1/2" x 23"
	solid	Use remaining white and black fabrics

Emblem

	Size	**Use**
C – White	1 – 8" x 8"	Star
	2 – 4" x 14"	Letters
H – Black	2 – 7" x 18"	Letters Backgrounds
	2 – 18" x 18"	Star Background
G – Gold	134" of 1 5/8" bias (see page 7 for cutting)	

Instructions given are for a Lap/Wall size quilt. If you wish to make a Queen size quilt, contact the author, Vicki Lynn Oehlke. Phone: 701-662-6795 or email: willowberry@gondtc.com

Army

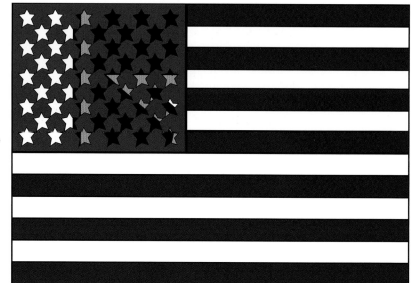

Constructing the Flag

The first step in creating your quilt is to construct the flag. This section will take you step-by-step through the process for the Army quilt.

Appliquéing the Stars

Trace 50 stars on paper side of fusible web.

Press stars to **wrong side** of fabric before cutting them out.

Refer to the "Stars Needed" chart, page 41, to find the number of star types for the Army emblem.

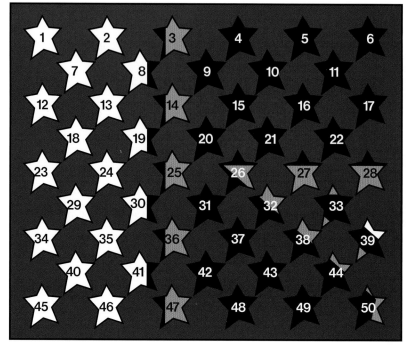

Star Placement Guide

For accurate star placement, refer to the full-size template found at the back of the book.

Stars Needed

White 14	Double Pieced 14	Triple Pieced 1	Black 18

Appliquéd Stars

Appliquéd:

3 1 Black Star Base with Gold Appliqué
2 Gold Star Base with Black Appliqué

Trace reversed image of stars, below.

Star Number	Whole Star Base	Appliqué Over Base
26	Black	Gold
33	Gold	Black
50	Gold	Black

- See instructions on page 42 on how to cut and place appliquéd stars.

Templates for appliquéd stars are reversed for cutting

26 33 50

Templates for pieced stars are reversed for cutting

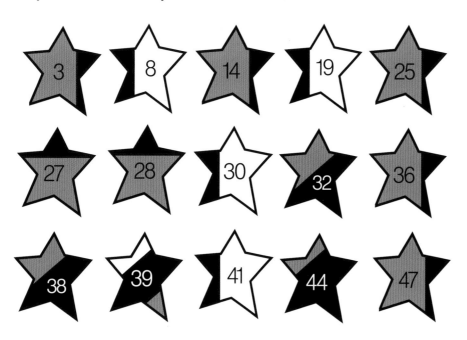

3 8 14 19 25

27 28 30 32 36

38 39 41 44 47

Preparing Pieced Stars:

Placing right sides together, **sew** the **pieced star strips**, **lengthwise** as shown, using a 1/4" seam allowance.

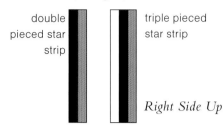

double pieced star strip

triple pieced star strip

Right Side Up

Press seams open and **trim** seams to 1/8" or less.

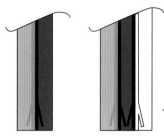

Trim Seam Allowance

Refer to "Stars Needed" chart (see page 41) and press the number of stars needed to wrong side of fabric. **Align seams** with lines on star templates.

Cut stars out on drawn line.

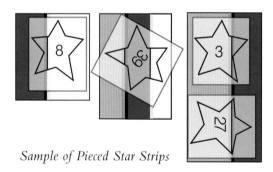

Sample of Pieced Star Strips

Follow star placement guide, page 40, to arrange your stars on the blue star background.

Press stars in place.
Stitch around stars by hand or machine. See various stitches on page 7 for stitching ideas.

Preparing Appliquéd Stars:

- Use one of the fusible web stars you traced.
- Press onto the wrong side of fabric listed under "whole star base" (see chart on page 41).
- Cut around "whole star base" on the line.

important: Be sure to leave the fusible web paper on until instructed to remove.

- Trace the shape of the "appliqué over base" star on paper side of fusible web.

- Press onto wrong side of fabric indicated in "appliqué over base" column.

- Cut out "appliqué over base" star piece.

- Turn "whole star base" right side up. Place and press star pieces onto the "whole star base".

- Trim whole star around edges if necessary.
- Now, you can remove the paper backing from the "whole star base" position and press onto the blue star background along with the other 49 stars.
- Straight stitch close to the edges of the "appliqué over base" with small stitches. Use the same colored thread as the "appliqué over base" fabric.

Piecing the Flag

note: Use a slightly longer stitch than usual as you will be ripping out large portions of these seams later. Use a regular stitch length if you don't plan to add one of the emblems.

Sew the 4 shorter red strips and 3 shorter white strips together as in diagram.

Press seams toward Red.

Sew the red & white unit to the right side of the blue background with appliquéd stars.

Press seam toward Blue.

Sew the 3 longer white strips and the 3 longer red strips together as in diagram.

Press seams toward Red.

Sew this unit to the bottom of the stars and stripes unit.

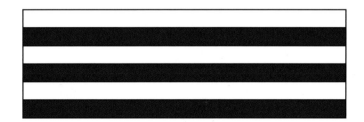

Press seam toward Red/Blue.

Flag measures:
13 1/2" x 21 1/2"

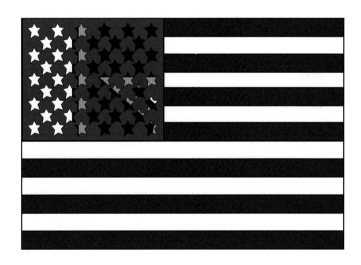

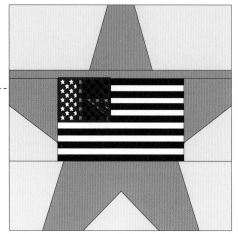

Army

Constructing the Large Background Star

The second step in creating your quilt is to construct the large background star. This section will take you step-by-step through the process for the Army quilt.

Step 1: Preparing Background and Large Star Pieces
Measure, mark and cut from **mark to corner** as shown in diagrams with a **dotted line**.

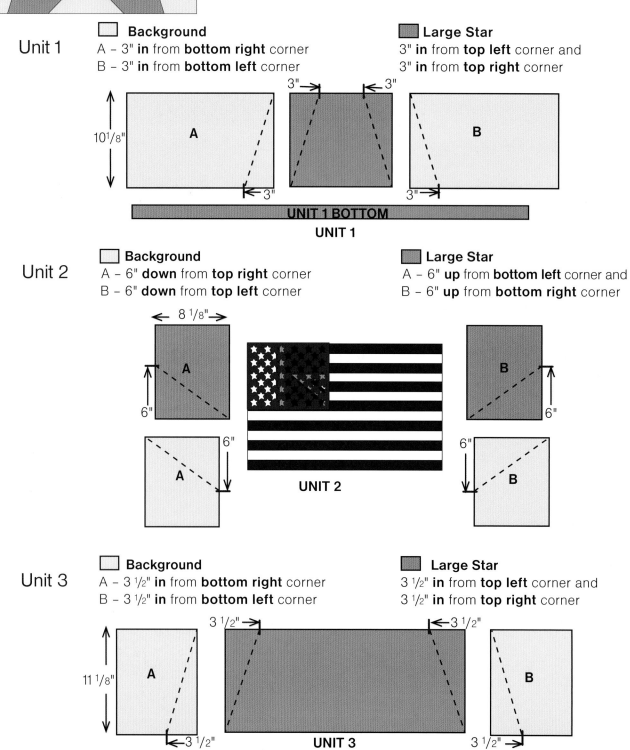

Unit 1

Background
A – 3" **in** from **bottom right** corner
B – 3" **in** from **bottom left** corner

Large Star
3" **in** from **top left** corner and
3" **in** from **top right** corner

10 1/8" 3" → ← 3" A B ← 3" 3" →

UNIT 1 BOTTOM

UNIT 1

Unit 2

Background
A – 6" **down** from **top right** corner
B – 6" **down** from **top left** corner

Large Star
A – 6" **up** from **bottom left** corner and
B – 6" **up** from **bottom right** corner

← 8 1/8" → A 6" B 6" 6" A B 6"

UNIT 2

Unit 3

Background
A – 3 1/2" **in** from **bottom right** corner
B – 3 1/2" **in** from **bottom left** corner

Large Star
3 1/2" **in** from **top left** corner and
3 1/2" **in** from **top right** corner

11 1/8" 3 1/2" → ← 3 1/2" A B ← 3 1/2" 3 1/2" →

UNIT 3

Step 2: Pinning And Sewing

Pin And Sew Unit 1

Join Unit 1A background to **left side** of **Unit 1** large star.

Join Unit 1B background to **right side** of **Unit 1** large star.

Sew Unit 1 bottom large star tan to **bottom** of the **above joined units**.

Press toward **tan strip**.

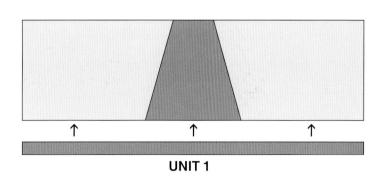

UNIT 1

Pin And Sew Unit 2

Join Unit 2A background to **Unit 2A** large star.

Join Unit 2B background to **Unit 2B** large star.

Sew Unit 2A to the **left side** of your **flag**.

Sew Unit 2B to the **right side** of your **flag**.

Press toward large star.

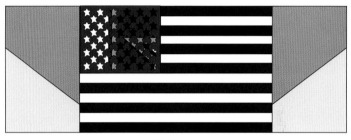

UNIT 2

Pin And Sew Unit 3

Join Unit 3A background to the **left side** of **Unit 3** large star.

Join Unit 3B background to the **right side** of **Unit 3** large star.

Press toward large star.

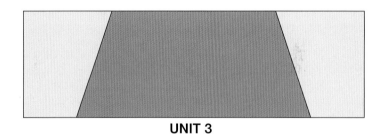

UNIT 3

Appliqué Unit 3C

Lay Unit 3C background star pieces **right sides together**.

Mark center of the 14 1/8" top edge.

Cut triangle
- Line up ruler from center mark to bottom right corner. Cut.
- Line up ruler from center mark to bottom left corner. Cut.

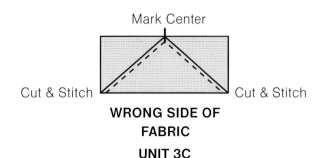

Mark Center

Cut & Stitch   Cut & Stitch

WRONG SIDE OF FABRIC

UNIT 3C

Prepare for appliqué
- Sew the two sides just cut.
- Trim top point.
- Turn right side out.
- Press.

Center appliqué
- Press pieced Unit 3 in half by lining up the two seams.
- Lay Unit 3 flat, right side up.
- Line up raw edge of triangle with the bottom edge of pieced Unit 3, and the **point** of the triangle with the pressed **crease**.
- Pin and stitch triangle to large star fabric by hand or machine.

Trim out the two layers of excess fabric from the back if you wish.

UNIT 3

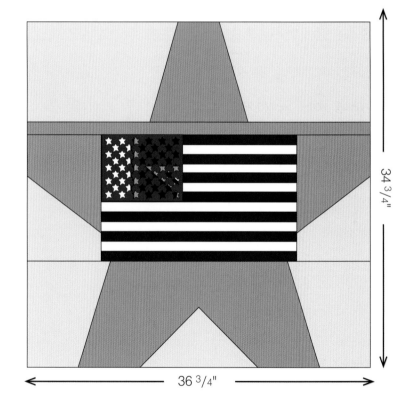

UNIT 3C

Center & Appliqué

Step 3 - Joining Units

Line up the **center of the top star point** (Unit 1 – bottom edge) with the **center of the flag** (Unit 2 – top edge).

Lay flat and **pin seam** from center out.

Stitch Unit 1 to **Unit 2**.

Press seam toward the **flag**.

Line up the **flag center** (bottom edge) with the **center crease of Unit 3**.

Lay flat and **pin seam** from center out.

Stitch and **press** toward **flag**.

Trim finished quilt center if necessary.

34 3/4"

36 3/4"

Adding an Emblem

The third step in creating your quilt is to add an emblem. This section will take you step-by-step through the process for the Army quilt.

ṉote: Find the emblem templates in the back of your book.

Sewing the Emblem

Prepare Appliqué:
ṉote: Trace the emblem from the templates located in the back of your book.

See General Instructions on page 6 for detailed description of how to prepare the appliqué.

Using the template found in the back of the book, **trace** emblem piece to paper side (dull side) of freezer paper. **Lay** fabrics cut for each emblem section with **right sides together**. **Press** and **pin** each traced section onto corresponding fabric. **Sew** on the line **leaving raw edges open** where indicated. **Remove paper. Trim excess** fabric leaving 1/8" to 1/4" seam allowance. **Clip** curves and points.

Turning Your Sewn Appliqué Pieces:
With wrong sides of fabric still out, **place** sewn emblem on top of the template. Make sure emblem is facing correct direction. **Cut** a slit in top layer of fabric. **Turn** and **press.**

Stitch or **press** on any small appliqué pieces indicated for your emblem.

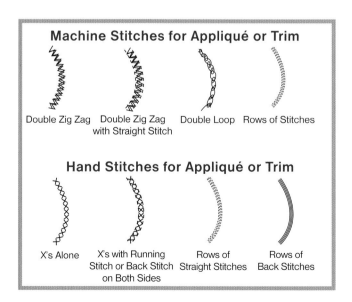

Prepare black backgrounds A and B.

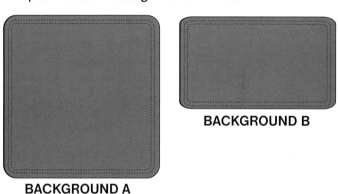

BACKGROUND B

BACKGROUND A

Prepare gold bias trim. See page 7 for preparing bias.

Using the emblem template found in the back of your book as a guide, appliqué gold bias trim around black background symbol pieces A and B.

Pin, Pin, Pin, Pin, Pin! in place following template.

ṉote: Appliqué by machine or by hand using thread to match fabric.

Corners
You may not like them when you're working on them but, you'll love the result.

Even with the bias, you will have to take some tucks on the inside edge.

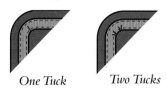

One Tuck   *Two Tucks*

White Star – Reverse Appliqué on Background A:

Trim black fabric from back of star emblem ¼ to ½ inch in from stitch line of appliquéd bias.

Back

Trace white star onto freezer paper.

Center on front of black square.

Press and pin in place.

Machine stitch on drawn line with black thread. This will mark the edges of your star.

Front

Remove paper and make slits in fabric from center of star into star points and inside angles as shown.

Trim away some of the black fabric in star area.

Baste white fabric square onto back.

Fold black fabric under along stitching and pin.

Straight stitch or **blanket stitch** around star –close to edge – with black thread on the black fabric.

Trim Star With Gold Bias:
Pin bias in place as you go.

You will trim excess and topstitch crease at point and edges of bias once you have the bias placed and pinned.

← Fold

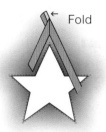

Continue around star folding at each inner and outer point.

Fold ends under, **trim** and **topstitch**.

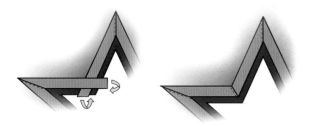

You will have to **tack** and **stitch** down bias at points and angles.

Trim away bias that is folded at points after topstitching point seams.

Topstitch around star on both edges of the gold bias.

U.S. ARMY Letters on Background B:
Follow instructions on page 47 to appliqué bias trim to background.

Trace letters onto feezer paper from the full-size template located in the back of your book. Follow "Prepare Appliqué" instructions on page 47. Pin in place and straight stitch close to edge of letters. Use white thread to match your fabric.

Appliqué this section of the emblem beneath the flag, after you have woven and stitched the main part of the emblem in place.

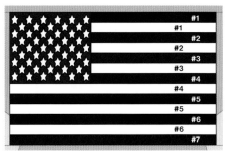

Numbered Stripes Chart

Weaving the Emblem

Position emblem piece(s) on the flag.

Follow emblem templates to center and position emblem piece(s).

Place a small gold safety pin in each seam of the flag where seam and emblem meet.

Pin emblem piece(s) in place leaving any part of the emblem below #6 red stripe loose.

Weave lower part of flag.
You will be weaving the emblem under the red stripe and over the white stripe.

Open top seam of red strip #7 between gold pins.

open seam

U.S.ARMY

Pull lower portion of emblem piece through seam to the back of the quilt center.

Lay quilt out flat so seam lies in place.

Pin seam.

Using matching red thread, sew seam closed with straight stitch close to edge of red stripe.

Trim away excess fabric of emblem covering star area of flag, leaving at least 1/2" overlap.

Weaving the Emblem

Remove straight pins.

Fold upper part of emblem down and open bottom seam of red stripe #6 between gold pins.

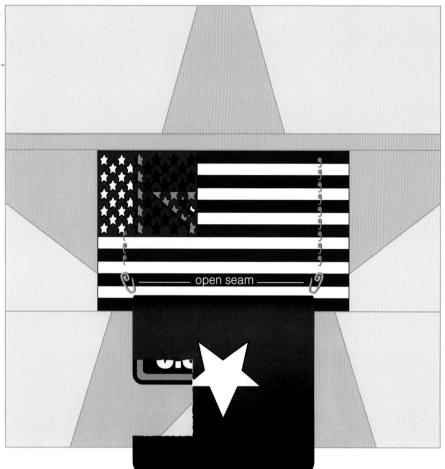

Pull emblem up through seam to back of flag.

Pin rest of emblem up to keep out of seam as you straight stitch seam closed as before.

Continue weaving the emblem into the lower portion of flag until emblem is brought up to the back of flag in the seam along the bottom of the blue star background and bottom of red stripe #4.

Use matching thread on both the blue and red fabrics as you straight stitch seam closed.

Weave under blue background of stars and upper stripes.

Open top seam of red stripe #4 between gold pins.

Open the seam of white stripe #3 and blue background of stars.

Bring emblem UP through seam to front of flag.

Weaving the Emblem

Emblems that weave under blue background:

Fold and pin emblem as shown in picture to keep emblem and stripes flat as you pin in place and sew along edge of red stripe with matching thread.

Leave seam of blue background and white stripe #3 open. You will sew this after emblem weaving is finished.

Open bottom seam of red stripe #3.

Bring emblem through to back. Topstitch seam closed as before.

Continue weaving in this manner until emblem is brought through the bottom seam of red stripe #1. Topstitch.

Open top seam of flag between gold pins.

Bring emblem up through seam to front of quilt.

Topstitch seam closed using matching blue and matching red thread.

Topstitch with matching blue thread along right side of blue background for stars to close the open seams.

Continue topstitching around blue background to make it uniform if you wish.

Finish edges of emblem.

Pin emblem edges to flag and background at open edges.

Topstitch emblem to quilt center using a stitch of your choice. See various stitches on page 7 for stitching ideas.

The last step in creating your quilt is adding the borders. See page 120 for detailed instructions for adding borders to finish your quilt.

Navy
yardage
Fabric requirements

See page 121 for yardage and cutting instructions for both options.

Lap/Wall Size 50" x 52"

Flag & Background Star

Colors	Yardage
A – Blue ....fat quarter	
B – Red .... $^1/4$ yard	
C – White .... $^1/3$ yard	
D – Background (includes outer border)...3 yards	
E – Large Star (Tan)................................1 $^1/4$ yards	
F – Inner Border ....1 $^1/3$ yards	

Emblem

G – Gold ....2 – 17" x 21"

You will have a crescent shape to sew and appliqué for cutout in top of anchor.

Binding & Backing

Binding... $^1/2$ yard
Backing..3 $^1/4$ yards

cutting
Cut in order

Flag

	Size	Use
A – Blue	1 – 7 $^1/2$" x 9"	Star Background
B – Red - first cut.....................	3 strips 1 $^1/2$" x 43"	Flag Stripes
from these cut..........	4 – 1 $^1/2$" x 13"	Flag Stripes
	3 – 1 $^1/2$" x 21 $^1/2$"	Flag Stripes
C – White - first cut...................	3 strips 1 $^1/2$" x 43"	Flag Stripes
from these cut	3 – 1 $^1/2$" x 13"	Flag Stripes
	3 – 1 $^1/2$" x 21 $^1/2$"	Flag Stripes

Background Star

	Size	Use
D – Background	2 – 10 $^1/8$" x 16 $^5/8$"	Unit 1
	2 – 9 $^5/8$" x 8 $^1/8$"	Unit 2
	2 – 11 $^1/8$" x 9 $^1/4$"	Unit 3
	2 – 6 $^1/8$" x 14 $^1/8$"	Unit 3C
E – Large Star (Tan)................	1 – 10 $^1/8$" x 11 $^1/8$"	Unit 1
	1 – 1 $^1/2$" x 37"	Unit 1 Bottom
	2 – 10 $^5/8$" x 8 $^1/8$"	Unit 2
	1 – 11 $^1/8$" x 26 $^3/4$"	Unit 3

Inner Border

Option 1 shown here. See page 121 for yardage and cutting instructions for both options.

Outer Border (OB)

	Size	Use
D – Background	lengthwise cut	
	2 – 5" x 54"	OB Top & Bottom
	2 – 5" x 43"	OB Sides
E – Large Star (Tan)................	2 – 5" x 7"	Top Star Point #1
	4 – 4" x 5"	Side Star Points #2 & #3
	4 – 6" x 7"	Bottom Star Points #4 & #5

Stars

	Star Type	Amounts
C – White	Pieced	1 – 1 $^1/4$" x 8"
G – Gold	Pieced	1 – 1 $^1/4$" x 8"
	Solid	Use remaining white and gold fabrics

Instructions given are for a Lap/Wall size quilt. If you wish to make a Queen size quilt, contact the author, Vicki Lynn Oehlke. Phone: 701-662-6795 or email: willowberry@gondtc.com

Navy

Constructing the Flag

The first step in creating your quilt is to construct the flag. This section will take you step-by-step through the process for the Navy quilt.

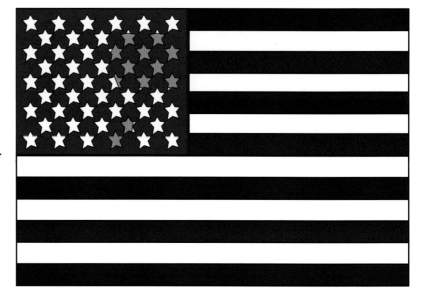

Appliquéing the Stars

Trace 50 stars on paper side of fusible web.

Press stars to **wrong side** of fabric before cutting them out.

Refer to the "Stars Needed" chart, page 59, to find the number of star types for the Navy emblem.

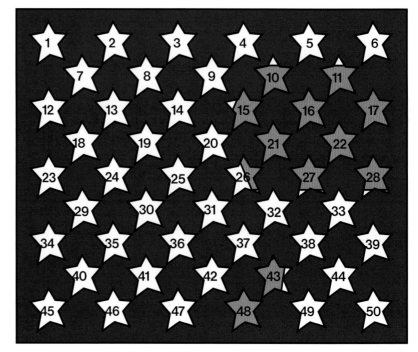

Star Placement Guide

For accurate star placement, refer to the full-size template found at the back of the book.

Stars Needed

White
38

Gold
5

Double Pieced
5

Appliquéd Stars

Appliquéd:
2   2 white star base with gold appliqué

Trace reversed image of stars, below.

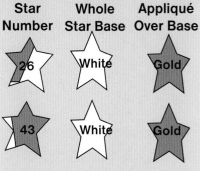

Star Number	Whole Star Base	Appliqué Over Base
26	White	Gold
43	White	Gold

- See instructions on page 60 to cut and place appliquéd stars.

Templates for appliquéd stars are reversed for cutting

Templates for pieced stars are reversed for cutting

Preparing Pieced Stars:

Placing right sides together, **sew** the **pieced star strips**, **lengthwise** as shown, using a 1/4" seam allowance.

double
pieced star
strip

Right Side Up

Press seams open and **trim** seams to 1/8" or less.

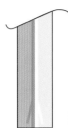

Trim Seam Allowance

Refer to "Stars Needed" chart (see page 59) and press the number of stars needed to wrong side of fabric. **Align seams** with lines on star templates.

Cut around the stars outline.

Sample of Pieced Star Strip

Follow star placement guide, page 58, to arrange your stars on the blue star background.

Press stars in place.
Stitch around stars by hand or machine. See various stitches on page 7 for stitching ideas.

Preparing Appliquéd Stars:

- Use one of the fusible web stars you traced.
- Press onto the wrong side of fabric listed under "whole star base" (see chart page 59).
- Cut around "whole star base" on the line.

important: Be sure to leave the fusible web paper on until instructed to remove.

- Trace the shape of the "appliqué over base" star on paper side of fusible web.

- Press onto wrong side of fabric indicated in "appliqué over base" column.

- Cut out "appliqué over base" star pieces.

- Turn "whole star base" right side up. Place and press star pieces onto the "whole star base".

- Trim whole star around edges if necessary.
- Now you can remove the paper backing from the "whole star base" position and press onto the blue star background along with the other 49 stars.
- Straight stitch close to the edges of the "appliqué over base" with small stitches. Use the same colored thread as the "appliqué over base" fabric.

Piecing the Flag

note: Use a slightly longer stitch than usual as you will be ripping out large portions of these seams later. Use a regular stitch length if you don't plan to add one of the emblems.

Sew the 4 shorter red strips and 3 shorter white strips together as in diagram.

Press seams toward Red.

Sew the red & white unit to the right side of the blue background with appliquéd stars.

Press seam toward Blue.

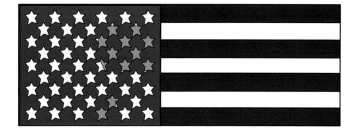

Sew the 3 longer white strips and the 3 longer red strips together as in diagram.

Press seams toward Red.

Sew this unit to the bottom of the stars and stripes unit.

Press seam toward Red/Blue.

Flag measures:
13 1/2" x 21 1/2"

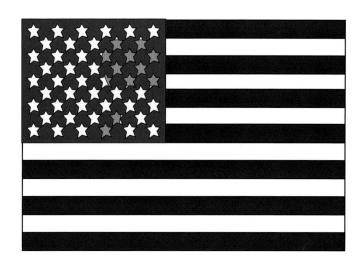

Constructing the Large Background Star

The second step in creating your quilt is to construct the large background star. This section will take you step-by-step through the process for the Navy quilt.

Step 1: Preparing Background and Large Star Pieces
Measure, mark and cut from **mark to corner** as shown in diagrams with a **dotted line**.

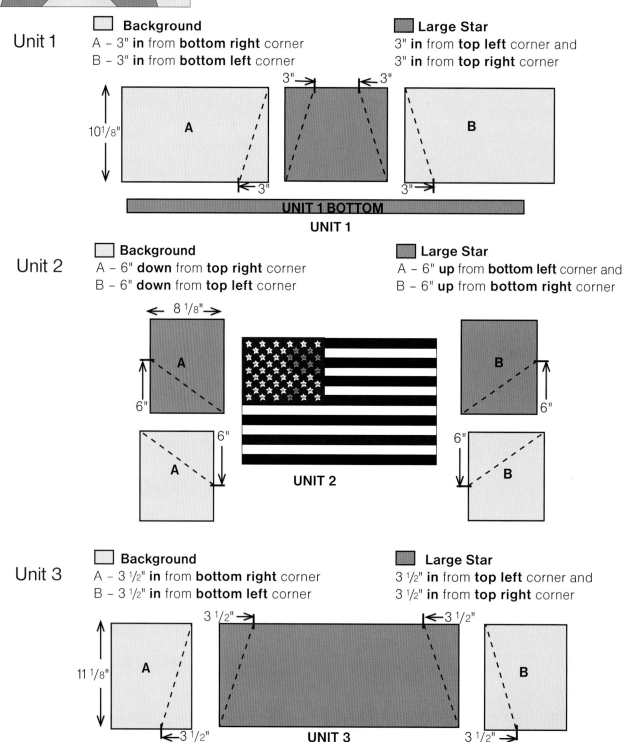

Unit 1

Background	Large Star
A – 3" **in** from **bottom right** corner	3" **in** from **top left** corner and
B – 3" **in** from **bottom left** corner	3" **in** from **top right** corner

Unit 2

Background	Large Star
A – 6" **down** from **top right** corner	A – 6" **up** from **bottom left** corner and
B – 6" **down** from **top left** corner	B – 6" **up** from **bottom right** corner

Unit 3

Background	Large Star
A – 3 1/2" **in** from **bottom right** corner	3 1/2" **in** from **top left** corner and
B – 3 1/2" **in** from **bottom left** corner	3 1/2" **in** from **top right** corner

Step 2: Pinning And Sewing

Pin And Sew Unit 1

Join Unit 1A background to **left side** of **Unit 1** large star.

Join Unit 1B background to **right side** of **Unit 1** large star.

Sew Unit 1 bottom large star tan to **bottom** of the **above joined units**.

Press toward **tan strip**.

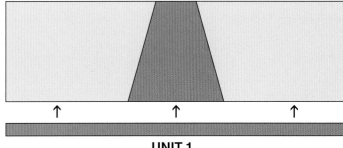

UNIT 1

Pin And Sew Unit 2

Join Unit 2A background to **Unit 2A** large star.

Join Unit 2B background to **Unit 2B** large star.

Sew Unit 2A to the **left side** of your **flag**.

Sew Unit 2B to the **right side** of your **flag**.

Press toward large star.

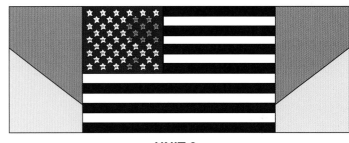

UNIT 2

Pin And Sew Unit 3

Join Unit 3A background to the **left side** of **Unit 3** large star.

Join Unit 3B background to the **right side** of **Unit 3** large star.

Press toward large star.

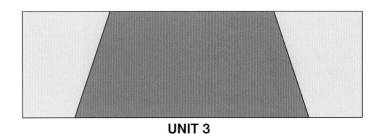

UNIT 3

Appliqué Unit 3C

Lay Unit 3C background star pieces **right sides together**.

Mark center of the 14 1/8" top edge.

Cut triangle
- Line up ruler from center mark to bottom right corner. Cut.
- Line up ruler from center mark to bottom left corner. Cut.

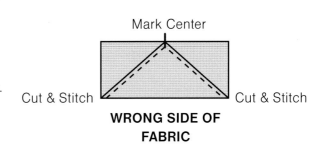

Mark Center

Cut & Stitch   Cut & Stitch

WRONG SIDE OF FABRIC

UNIT 3C

Prepare for appliqué
- Sew the two sides just cut.
- Trim top point.
- Turn right side out.
- Press.

Center appliqué
- Press pieced Unit 3 in half by lining up the two seams.
- Lay Unit 3 flat, right side up.
- Line up raw edge of triangle with the bottom edge of pieced Unit 3, and the **point** of the triangle with the pressed **crease**.
- Pin and stitch triangle to large star fabric by hand or machine.

Trim out the two layers of excess fabric from the back if you wish.

Step 3 - Joining Units

Line up the **center of the top star point** (Unit 1 – bottom edge) with the **center of the flag** (Unit 2 – top edge).

Lay flat and **pin seam** from center out.

Stitch Unit 1 to **Unit 2**.

Press seam toward the **flag**.

Line up the **flag center** (bottom edge) with the **center crease of Unit 3**.

Lay flat and **pin seam** from center out.

Stitch and **press** toward **flag**.

Trim finished quilt center if necessary.

UNIT 3

UNIT 3C

Center & Appliqué

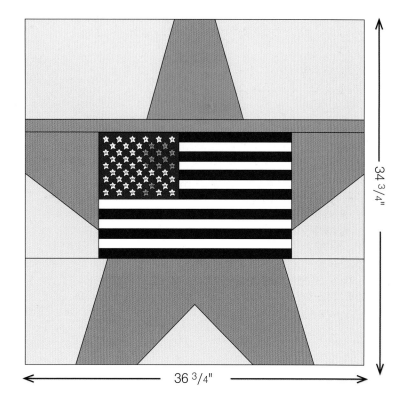

34 3/4"

36 3/4"

Adding an Emblem

The third step in creating your quilt is to add an emblem. This section will take you step-by-step through the process for the Navy quilt.

note: Find the emblem templates in the back of your book.

Sewing the Emblem

Prepare Appliqué:
note: Trace the emblem from the templates located in the back of your book.

See General Instructions on page 6 for detailed description of how to prepare the appliqué.

Refer to the template found in the back of the book for placement. **Trace** emblem piece to paper side (dull side) of freezer paper. **Lay** fabrics cut for each emblem section with **right sides together. Press** and **pin** each traced section onto corresponding fabric. **Sew** on the line **leaving raw edges open** where indicated.
Remove paper. Trim excess fabric leaving 1/8" to 1/4" seam allowance. **Clip** curves and points.

Turning Your Sewn Appliqué Pieces:
With wrong sides of fabric still out, **place** sewn emblem on top of the template. Make sure emblem is facing correct direction. **Cut** a slit in top layer of fabric. **Turn** and **press**.

Stitch or **press** on any small appliqué pieces indicated for your emblem.

Refer to the template for placement of any small appliqué pieces needed on your emblem and for placement in the flag.

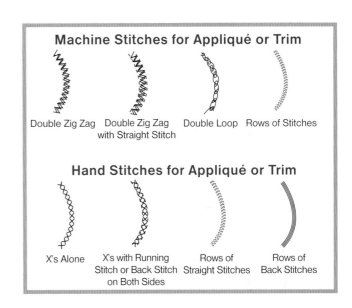

Machine Stitches for Appliqué or Trim

Double Zig Zag   Double Zig Zag   Double Loop   Rows of Stitches
                  with Straight Stitch

Hand Stitches for Appliqué or Trim

X's Alone   X's with Running   Rows of   Rows of
             Stitch or Back Stitch   Straight Stitches   Back Stitches
             on Both Sides

Small Appliqué Piece

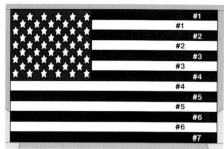

Numbered Stripes Chart

Weaving the Emblem

Position emblem piece(s) on the flag.

Follow emblem templates to center and position emblem piece(s).

Place a small gold safety pin in each seam of the flag where seam and emblem meet.

Pin emblem piece(s) in place leaving any part of the emblem below #6 red stripe loose.

Weave lower part of flag.
You will be weaving the emblem under the red stripe and over the white stripe.

Open top seam of red stripe #7 between gold pins.

open seam

Pull lower portion of emblem piece through seam to the back of the quilt center.

Lay quilt out flat so seam lies in place.

Pin seam.

Using matching red thread, sew seam closed with straight stitch close to edge of red stripe.

Open bottom seam of flag between gold pins.

Bring bottom of emblem UP through seam.

Sew seam closed as before.

open seam

Weaving the Emblem

Remove straight pins.

Fold upper part of emblem down and open bottom seam of red stripe #6 between gold pins.

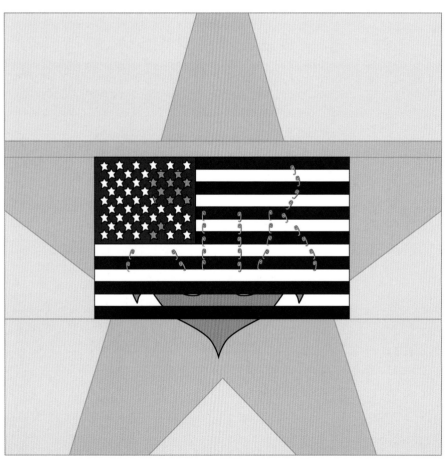

Pull emblem UP through seam to back of flag.

Pin rest of emblem up to keep out of seam as you straight stitch seam closed as before.

Continue weaving the emblem into the lower portion of flag until emblem is brought up to the back of flag in the seam along the bottom of the blue star background and bottom of red stripe #4.

Use matching thread on both the blue and red fabrics as you straight stitch seam closed.

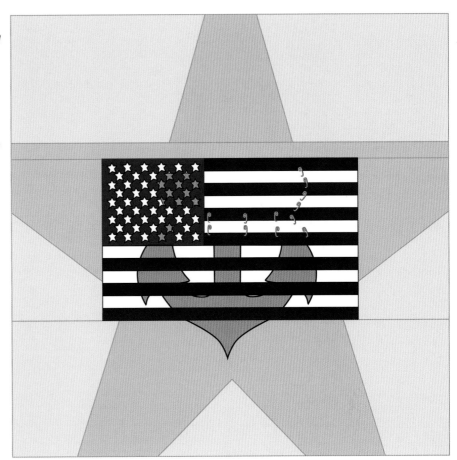

Weave under blue background of stars and upper stripes.

Open top seam of red stripe #4 between gold pins.

Bring emblem UP through seam to front of flag.

Open the seams of white stripes #1 and #2 and blue background of stars.

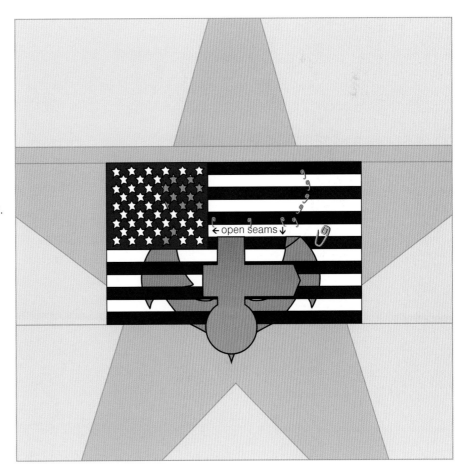

Weaving the Emblem

Emblems that weave under blue background:
Fold and pin emblem as shown in picture to keep emblem and stripes flat as you pin in place and sew along edge of red stripe with matching thread.

Leave seam of blue background and white stripes #1 and #2 open. You will sew this after emblem weaving is finished.

Open bottom seam of red stripe #3.

Bring emblem through to back. Topstitch seam closed as before.

Continue weaving in this manner until emblem is brought through the bottom seam of red stripe #1. Topstitch.

Open top seam of flag between gold pins.

Bring emblem up through seam to front of quilt.

Topstitch seam closed using matching blue and matching red thread.

Topstitch with matching blue thread along right side of blue background for stars to close the open seams.

Continue topstitching around blue background to make it uniform if you wish.

Finish edges of emblem.

Pin emblem edges to flag and background at open edges.

Topstitch emblem to quilt center using a stitch of your choice. See various stitches on page 7 for stitching ideas.

The last step in creating your quilt is adding the borders. See page 120 for detailed instructions for adding borders to finish your quilt.

Marines

yardage

Fabric requirements

Lap/Wall Size 50" x 52"

Flag & Background Star

Colors	Yardage
A – Blue	fat quarter
B – Red	1/4 yard
C – White	1/3 yard
D – Background (includes outer border)	3 yards
E – Large Star (Black)	1 1/4 yards
F – Inner Border	1 1/3 yards

Emblem

G – Gold	1 2/3 yards

Binding & Backing

Binding	1/2 yard
Backing	3 1/4 yards

cutting

Cut in order

Flag

	Size	Use
A – Blue	1 – 7 1/2" x 9"	Star Background
B – Red - first cut	3 strips 1 1/2" x 43"	Flag Stripes
from these cut	4 – 1 1/2" x 13"	Flag Stripes
	3 – 1 1/2" x 21 1/2"	Flag Stripes
C – White - first cut	3 strips 1 1/2" x 43"	Flag Stripes
from these cut	3 – 1 1/2" x 13"	Flag Stripes
	3 – 1 1/2" x 21 1/2"	Flag Stripes

Background Star

	Size	Use
D – Background	2 – 10 1/8" x 16 5/8"	Unit 1
	2 – 9 5/8" x 8 1/8"	Unit 2
	2 – 11 1/8" x 9 1/4"	Unit 3
	2 – 6 1/8" x 14 1/8"	Unit 3C
E – Large Star (Black)	1 – 10 1/8" x 11 1/8"	Unit 1
	1 – 1 1/2" x 37"	Unit 1 Bottom
	2 – 10 5/8" x 8 1/8"	Unit 2
	1 – 11 1/8" x 26 3/4"	Unit 3

Inner Border

Option 1 shown here. See page 121 for yardage and cutting instructions for both options.

Outer Border (OB)

	Size	Use
D – Background	lengthwise cut	
	2 – 5" x 54"	OB Top & Bottom
	2 – 5" x 43"	OB Sides
E – Large Star (Black)	2 – 5" x 7"	Top Star Point #1
	4 – 4" x 5"	Side Star Points #2 & #3
	4 – 6" x 7"	Bottom Star Points #4 & #5

Stars

	Star Type	Amounts
C – White	Pieced	1 – 1 1/2" x 24"
G – Gold	Pieced	1 – 1 1/2" x 24"
Solid Stars	Use remaining white and gold fabrics	

Emblem

	Size	Use
G – Gold	2 – 17" x 23"	Eagle
	2 – 11" x 14"	Emblem Top A
	2 – 10" x 18"	Emblem Bottom B

You will have two small shapes to sew and appliqué for cut outs in anchor top.

Instructions given are for a Lap/Wall size quilt. If you wish to make a Queen size quilt, contact the author, Vicki Lynn Oehlke. Phone: 701-662-6795 or email: willowberry@gondtc.com

Marines

Constructing the Flag

The first step in creating your quilt is to construct the flag. This section will take you step-by-step through the process for the Marines quilt.

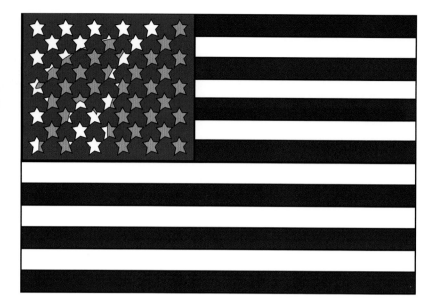

Appliquéing the Stars

Trace 50 stars on paper side of fusible web.

Press stars to **wrong side** of fabric before cutting them out.

Refer to the "Stars Needed" chart, page 75, to find the number of star types for the Marine emblem.

Star Placement Guide

For accurate star placement, refer to the full-size template found at the back of the book.

Stars Needed

 White
10

 Gold
22

Double Pieced
14

Appliquéd Stars

23 **30** **35** **36**

Appliquéd:
4 2 gold star with white appliqué
2 white star with gold appliqué
Trace reversed image of stars, below.

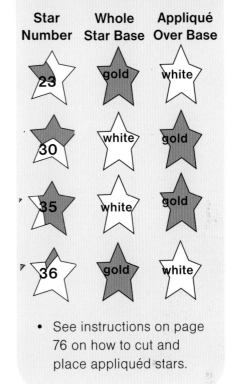

Star Number	Whole Star Base	Appliqué Over Base
23	gold	white
30	white	gold
35	white	gold
36	gold	white

• See instructions on page 76 on how to cut and place appliquéd stars.

Templates for appliquéd stars are reversed for cutting

23 30 35 36

Templates for pieced stars are reversed for cutting

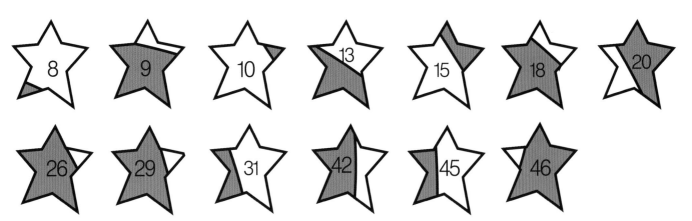

8 9 10 13 15 18 20

26 29 31 42 45 46

Preparing Pieced Stars:

Placing right sides together, **sew** the **pieced star strips**, **lengthwise** as shown, using a 1/4" seam allowance.

double
pieced star
strip

Right Side Up

Press seams open and **trim** seams to 1/8" or less.

Trim Seam Allowance

Refer to "Stars Needed" chart, page 75, and press the number of stars needed to wrong side of fabric. **Align seams** with lines on star templates.

Cut around the stars outline.

Sample of Pieced Star Strips

Follow star placement guide, page 75, to arrange your stars on the blue star background.

Press stars in place.
Stitch around stars by hand or machine. See various stitches on page 7 for stitching ideas.

Preparing Appliquéd Stars:

- Use one of the fusible web stars you traced.
- Press onto the wrong side of fabric listed under "whole star base" (see chart page 75).
- Cut around "whole star base" on the line.

important: Be sure to leave the fusible web paper on until instructed to remove.

- Trace the shape of the "appliqué over base" star on paper side of fusible web.

- Press onto wrong side of fabric indicated in "appliqué over base" column.

- Cut out "appliqué over base" star pieces.

- Turn "whole star base" right side up. Place and press star pieces onto the "whole star base".

- Trim whole star around edges if necessary.
- Now you can remove the paper backing from the "whole star base" position and press onto the blue star background along with the other 49 stars.
- Straight stitch close to the edges of the "appliqué over base" with small stitches. Use the same colored thread as the "appliqué over base" fabric.

Piecing the Flag

note: Use a slightly longer stitch than usual as you will be ripping out large portions of these seams later. Use a regular stitch length if you don't plan to add one of the emblems.

Sew the 4 shorter red strips and 3 shorter white strips together as in diagram.

Press seams toward Red.

Sew the red & white unit to the right side of the blue background with appliquéd stars.

Press seam toward Blue.

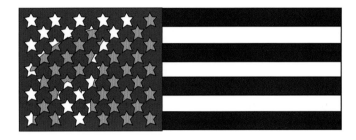

Sew the 3 longer white strips and the 3 longer red strips together as in diagram.

Press seams toward Red.

Sew this unit to the bottom of the stars and stripes unit.

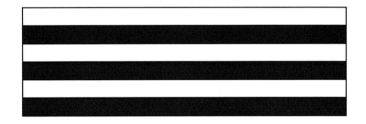

Press seam toward Red/Blue.

Flag measures:
13 1/2" x 21 1/2"

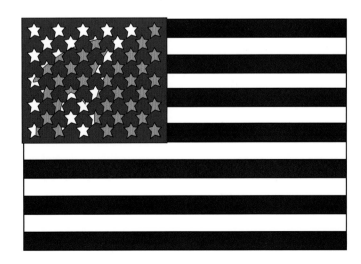

Constructing the Large Background Star

The second step in creating your quilt is to construct the large background star. This section will take you step-by-step through the process for the Marines quilt.

Step 1: Preparing Background and Large Star Pieces
Measure, mark and cut from **mark to corner** as shown in diagrams with a **dotted line**.

Unit 1

▢ **Background**
A – 3" **in** from **bottom right** corner
B – 3" **in** from **bottom left** corner

◼ **Large Star**
3" **in** from **top left** corner and
3" **in** from **top right** corner

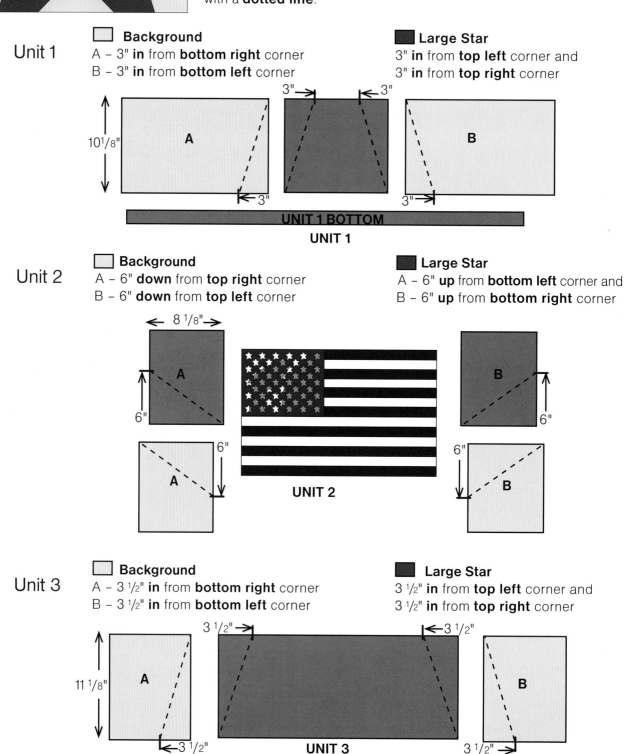

Step 2: Pinning And Sewing

Pin And Sew Unit 1

Join **Unit 1A** background to **left side** of **Unit 1** large star.

Join **Unit 1B** background to **right side** of **Unit 1** large star.

Sew **Unit 1 bottom** large star black to **bottom** of the **above joined units**.

Press toward **black strip**.

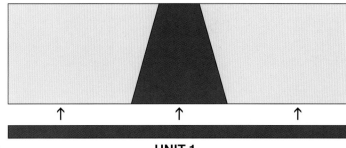

UNIT 1

Pin And Sew Unit 2

Join **Unit 2A** background to **Unit 2A** large star.

Join **Unit 2B** background to **Unit 2B** large star.

Sew **Unit 2A** to the **left side** of your **flag**.

Sew **Unit 2B** to the **right side** of your **flag**.

Press toward large star.

UNIT 2

Pin And Sew Unit 3

Join **Unit 3A** background to the **left side** of **Unit 3** large star.

Join **Unit 3B** background to the **right side** of **Unit 3** large star.

Press toward large star.

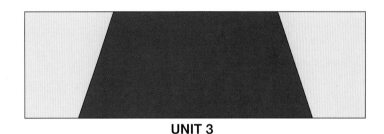

UNIT 3

Appliqué Unit 3C

Lay **Unit 3C** background star pieces **right sides together**.

Mark center of the 14 ⅛" top edge.

Cut triangle
- Line up ruler from center mark to bottom right corner. Cut.
- Line up ruler from center mark to bottom left corner. Cut.

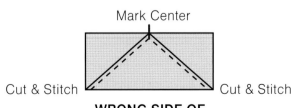

Mark Center

Cut & Stitch   Cut & Stitch

**WRONG SIDE OF
FABRIC
UNIT 3C**

Prepare for appliqué
- Sew the two sides just cut.
- Trim top point.
- Turn right side out.
- Press.

Center appliqué
- Press pieced Unit 3 in half by lining up the two seams.
- Lay Unit 3 flat, right side up.
- Line up raw edge of triangle with the bottom edge of pieced Unit 3, and the **point** of the triangle with the pressed **crease**.
- Pin and stitch triangle to large star fabric by hand or machine.

Trim out the two layers of excess fabric from the back if you wish.

Step 3 - Joining Units

Line up the **center of the top star point** (Unit 1 – bottom edge) with the **center of the flag** (Unit 2 – top edge).

Lay flat and **pin seam** from center out.

Stitch Unit 1 to **Unit 2.**

Press seam toward the **flag**.

Line up the **flag center** (bottom edge) with the **center crease of Unit 3.**

Lay flat and **pin seam** from center out.

Stitch and **press** toward **flag**.

Trim finished quilt center if necessary.

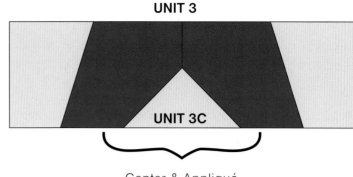

UNIT 3

UNIT 3C

Center & Appliqué

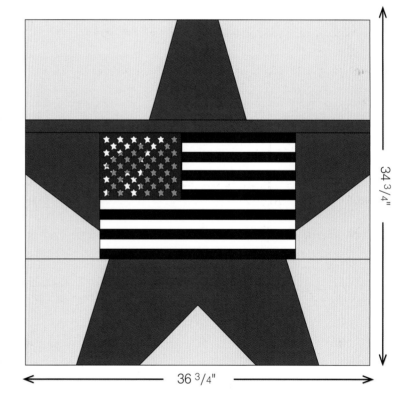

34 3/4"

36 3/4"

Adding an Emblem

The third step in creating your quilt is to add an emblem. This section will take you step-by-step through the process for the Marines quilt.

note: Find the emblem templates in the back of your book.

Sewing the Emblem

Prepare Appliqué:

note: Trace the emblem from the templates located in the back of your book.

See General Instructions on page 6 for detailed description of how to prepare the appliqué.

Refer to the template found in the back of the book for placement. **Trace** emblem piece to paper side (dull side) of freezer paper. **Lay** fabrics cut for each emblem section with **right sides together**. **Press** and **pin** each traced section onto corresponding fabric. **Sew** on the line **leaving raw eges open** where indicated.
Remove paper. **Trim excess** fabric leaving 1/8" to 1/4" seam allowance. **Clip** curves and points.

Turning Your Sewn Appliqué Pieces:

With wrong sides of fabric still out, **place** sewn emblem on top of the template. Make sure emblem is facing correct direction. **Cut** a slit in top layer of fabric. **Turn** and **press**.

Stitch or **press** on any small appliqué pieces indicated for your emblem.

Refer to the template for placement of any small appliqué pieces needed on your emblem and for placement in the flag.

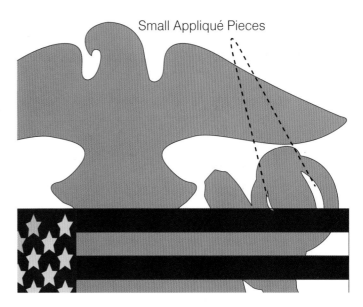

Small Appliqué Pieces

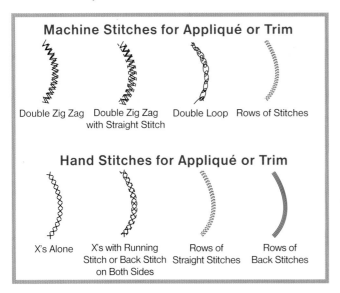

Machine Stitches for Appliqué or Trim

Double Zig Zag

Double Zig Zag with Straight Stitch

Double Loop

Rows of Stitches

Hand Stitches for Appliqué or Trim

X's Alone

X's with Running Stitch or Back Stitch on Both Sides

Rows of Straight Stitches

Rows of Back Stitches

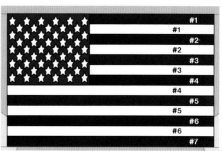

Numbered Stripes Chart

Weaving the Emblem

Position emblem piece(s) on the flag.

Follow emblem templates to center and position emblem piece(s).

Place a small gold safety pin in each seam of the flag where seam and emblem meet.

Pin emblem piece(s) in place leaving any part of the emblem below #6 red stripe loose.

Weave lower part of flag.
You will be weaving the emblem under the red stripe and over the white stripe.

Open top seam of red stripe #7 between gold pins.

Pull lower portion of emblem piece through seam to the back of the quilt center.

Lay quilt out flat so seam lies in place.

Pin seam.

Using matching red thread, sew seam closed with straight stitch close to edge of red stripe.

Open bottom seam of flag between gold pins.

Bring bottom of emblem UP through seam.

Sew seam closed as before.

Weaving the Emblem

Remove straight pins.

Fold upper part of emblem down and open bottom seam of red stripe #6 between gold pins.

Pull emblem up through seam to back of flag.

Pin rest of emblem up to keep out of seam as you straight stitch seam closed as before.

Continue weaving the emblem into the lower portion of flag until emblem is brought up to the back of flag in the seam along the bottom of the blue star background and bottom of red stripe #4.

Use matching thread on both the blue and red fabrics as you straight stitch seam closed.

Weave under blue background of stars and upper stripes.

Open top seam of red stripe #4 between gold pins.

Open the seam of white stripe #3 and blue background of stars.

Bring raw edge of emblem top DOWN through seam to back of flag.

Weaving the Emblem

Emblems that weave under blue background:

Fold and pin emblem as shown in picture to keep emblem and stripes flat as you pin in place and sew along edge of red stripe with matching thread.

Leave seam of blue background and white stripe #3 open. We will sew this after emblem weaving is finished.

Open bottom seam of red stripe #3.

Bring emblem through to back. Topstitch seam closed as before.

Continue weaving in this manner until emblem is brought through the bottom seam of red stripe #1. Topstitch.

Open top seam of flag between gold pins.

Bring emblem up through seam to front of quilt.

Topstitch seam closed using matching blue and matching red thread.

Topstitch with matching blue thread along right side of blue background for stars to close the open seams.

Continue topstitching around blue background to make it uniform if you wish.

Finish edges of emblem.

Pin emblem edges to flag and background at open edges.

Topstitch emblem to quilt center using a stitch of your choice. See various stitches on page 7 for stitching ideas.

The last step in creating your quilt is adding the borders. See page 120 for detailed instructions for adding borders to finish your quilt.

Air Force
yardage
Fabric requirements

Lap/Wall Size 50" x 52"

Flag & Background Star

Colors	Yardage
A – Blue	fat quarter
B – Red	1/4 yard
C – White	1/3 yard
D – Background (includes outer border)	3 yards
E – Large Star (Cream Print)	1 1/4 yards
F – Inner Border	1 1/3 yards

Emblem

A – Blue	1 fat quarter
G – Gold	2/3 yard

You will have an oval of gold to sew and appliqué for center of star

Binding & Backing

Binding	1/2 yard
Backing	3 1/4 yards

cutting
Cut in order

Flag

	Size	Use
A – Blue	1 – 7 1/2" x 9"	Star Background
B – Red - first cut	3 strips 1 1/2" x 43"	Flag Stripes
from these cut	4 – 1 1/2" x 13"	Flag Stripes
	3 – 1 1/2" x 21 1/2"	Flag Stripes
C – White - first cut	3 strips 1 1/2" x 43"	Flag Stripes
from these cut	3 – 1 1/2" x 13"	Flag Stripes
	3 – 1 1/2" x 21 1/2"	Flag Stripes

Background Star

	Size	Use
D – Background	2 – 10 1/8" x 16 5/8"	Unit 1
	2 – 9 5/8" x 8 1/8"	Unit 2
	2 – 11 1/8" x 9 1/4"	Unit 3
	2 – 6 1/8" x 14 1/8"	Unit 3C
E – Large Star (Cream Print)	1 – 10 1/8" x 11 1/8"	Unit 1
	1 – 1 1/2" x 37"	Unit 1 Bottom
	2 – 10 5/8" x 8 1/8"	Unit 2
	1 – 11 1/8" x 26 3/4"	Unit 3

Inner Border

Option 1 shown here. See page 121 for yardage and cutting instructions for both options.

Outer Border (OB)

	Size	Use
D – Background (Light Print) . lengthwise cut		
	2 – 5" x 54"	OB Top & Bottom
	2 – 5" x 43"	OB Sides
E – Large Star (Cream Print)	2 – 5" x 7"	Top Star Point #1
	4 – 4" x 5"	Side Star Points #2 & #3
	4 – 6" x 7"	Bottom Star Points #4 & #5

Stars

	Star Type	Amounts
C – White	Pieced	1 – 2" x 18"
G – Gold	Pieced	1 – 2" x 18"
Solid Stars		Use remaining white and gold fabrics

Emblem

	Size	Use
A – Blue	2 – 7" x 7"	Star
G – Gold	2 – 16" x 20"	A & B of Emblem
	2 – 3" x 4"	Wing Tip

You will have an oval of gold to sew and appliqué for center of star.

Instructions given are for a Lap/Wall size quilt. If you wish to make a Queen size quilt, contact the author, Vicki Lynn Oehlke.
Phone: 701-662-6795
or email:
willowberry@gondtc.com

Air Force

Constructing the Flag

The first step in creating your quilt is to construct the flag. This section will take you step-by-step through the process for the Air Force quilt.

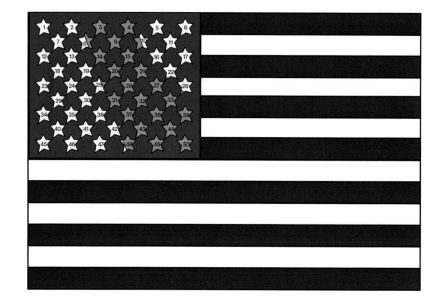

Appliquéing the Stars

Trace 50 stars on paper side of fusible web.

Press stars to **wrong side** of fabric before cutting them out. Leave fusible web on until instructed to remove.

Refer to the "Stars Needed" chart, page 91, to find the number of star types for the Air Force emblem.

Star Placement Guide

For accurate star placement, refer to the full-size template found at the back of the book.

Stars Needed

White	Gold	Pieced
25	19	6

Templates for pieced stars are reversed for cutting

Preparing Pieced Stars:

Placing right sides together, **sew** the **pieced star strips**, **lengthwise** as shown, using a 1/4" seam allowance.

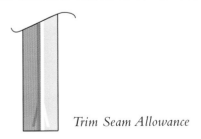

Right Side Up

Press seams open and **trim** seams to 1/8" or less.

Trim Seam Allowance

Refer to "Stars Needed" chart (above) and press the number of stars needed to wrong side of fabric. **Align seams** with lines on star templates.

Sample of Pieced Star Strips

Cut stars out on the drawn line. Remove fusible web backing.

Follow star placement guide, page 90, to arrange your stars on the blue star background.

Press stars in place.
Stitch around stars by hand or machine. See various stitches on page 7 for stitching ideas.

Piecing the Flag

note: Use a slightly longer stitch than usual as you will be ripping out large portions of these seams later. Use a regular stitch length if you don't plan to add one of the emblems.

Sew the 4 shorter red strips and 3 shorter white strips together as in diagram.

Press seams toward Red.

Sew the red & white unit to the right side of the blue background with appliquéd stars.

Press seam toward Blue.

Sew the 3 longer white strips and the 3 longer red strips together as in diagram.

Press seams toward Red.

Sew this unit to the bottom of the stars and stripes unit.

Press seam toward Red/Blue.

Flag measures:
13 1/2" x 21 1/2"

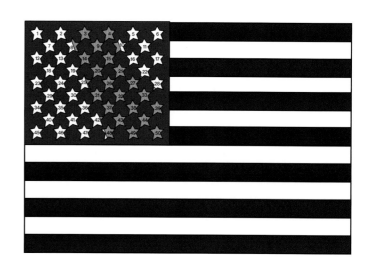

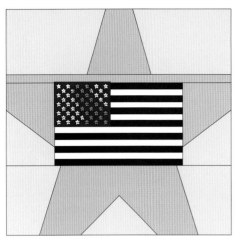

Constructing the Large Background Star

The second step in creating your quilt is to construct the large background star. This section will take you step-by-step through the process for the Air Force quilt.

Step 1: Preparing Background and Large Star Pieces
Measure, mark and cut from mark to corner as shown in diagrams with a dotted line.

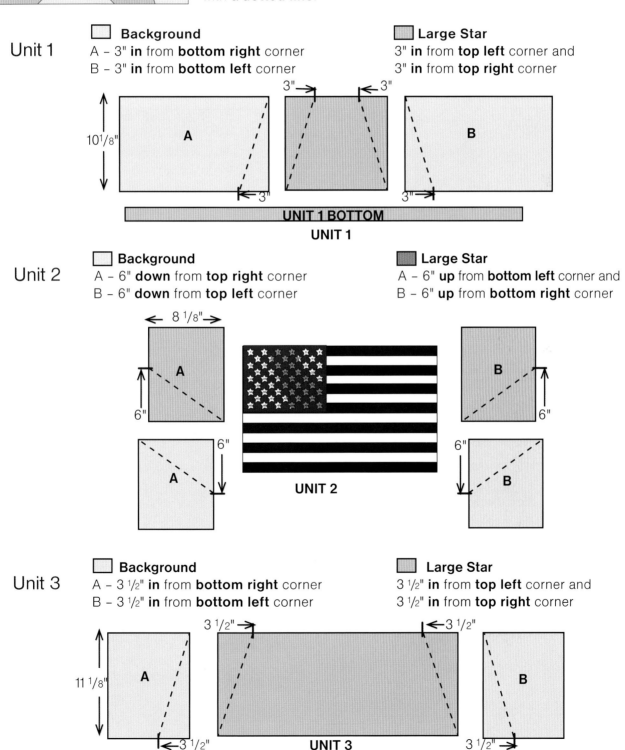

Unit 1

◻ **Background**
A – 3" **in** from **bottom right** corner
B – 3" **in** from **bottom left** corner

▨ **Large Star**
3" **in** from **top left** corner and
3" **in** from **top right** corner

10 1/8"

A

3"   3"

B

3"   3"

UNIT 1 BOTTOM

UNIT 1

Unit 2

◻ **Background**
A – 6" **down** from **top right** corner
B – 6" **down** from **top left** corner

▨ **Large Star**
A – 6" **up** from **bottom left** corner and
B – 6" **up** from **bottom right** corner

← 8 1/8" →

A   6"

B   6"

A   6"

B   6"

UNIT 2

Unit 3

◻ **Background**
A – 3 1/2" **in** from **bottom right** corner
B – 3 1/2" **in** from **bottom left** corner

▨ **Large Star**
3 1/2" **in** from **top left** corner and
3 1/2" **in** from **top right** corner

11 1/8"

3 1/2"   3 1/2"

A

B

3 1/2"   3 1/2"

UNIT 3

Step 2: Pinning And Sewing

Pin And Sew Unit 1

Join Unit 1A background to **left side** of **Unit 1** large star.

Join Unit 1B background to **right side** of **Unit 1** large star.

Sew Unit 1 bottom large star cream print to **bottom** of the **above joined units**.

Press toward **cream print strip**.

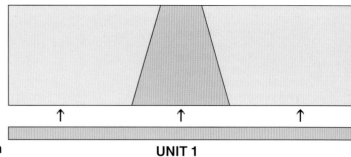

UNIT 1

Pin And Sew Unit 2

Join Unit 2A background to **Unit 2A** large star.

Join Unit 2B background to **Unit 2B** large star.

Sew Unit 2 A to the **left side** of your **flag**.

Sew Unit 2 B to the **right side** of your **flag**.

Press toward large star.

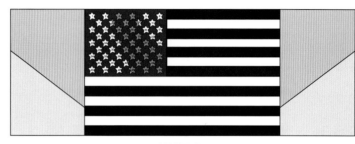

UNIT 2

Pin And Sew Unit 3

Join Unit 3A background to the **left side** of **Unit 3** large star.

Join Unit 3B background to the **right side** of **Unit 3** large star.

Press toward large star.

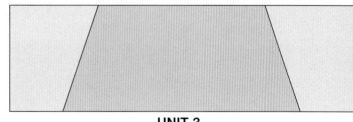

UNIT 3

Appliqué Unit 3C

Lay Unit 3C background star pieces **right sides together**.

Mark center of the 14 1/8" top edge.

Cut triangle
- Line up ruler from center mark to bottom right corner. Cut.
- Line up ruler from center mark to bottom left corner. Cut.

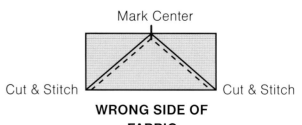

Mark Center

Cut & Stitch   Cut & Stitch

WRONG SIDE OF FABRIC

UNIT 3C

Prepare for appliqué

- Sew the two sides just cut.
- Trim top point.
- Turn right side out.
- Press.

Center appliqué

- Press pieced Unit 3 in half by lining up the two seams.
- Lay Unit 3 flat, right side up.
- Line up raw edge of triangle with the bottom edge of pieced Unit 3, and the **point** of the triangle with the pressed **crease**.
- Pin and stitch triangle to large star fabric by hand or machine.

Trim out the two layers of excess fabric from the back if you wish.

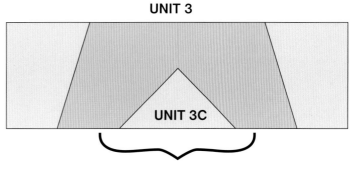

UNIT 3

Center & Appliqué

Step 3 - Joining Units

Line up the **center of the top star point** (Unit 1 – bottom edge) with the **center of the flag** (Unit 2 – top edge).

Lay flat and **pin seam** from center out.

Stitch Unit 1 to **Unit 2**.

Press seam toward the **flag**.

Line up the **flag center** (bottom edge) with the **center crease of Unit 3**.

Lay flat and **pin seam** from center out.

Stitch and **press** toward **flag**.

Trim finished quilt center if necessary.

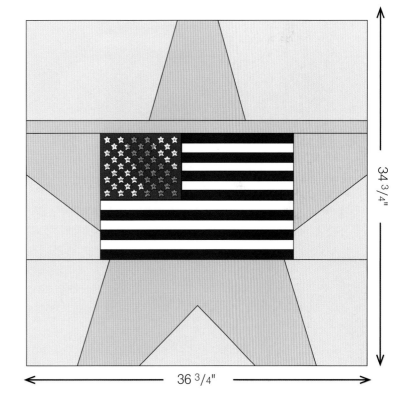

34 3/4"

36 3/4"

Air Force

Adding an Emblem

The third step in creating your quilt is to add an emblem. This section will take you step-by-step through the process for the Air Force quilt.

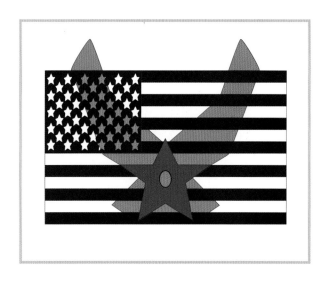

note: Find the emblem templates in the back of your book.

Sewing the Emblem

Prepare Appliqué:

note: Trace the emblem from the templates located in the back of your book.

See General Instructions on page 6 for detailed description of how to prepare the appliqué.

Refer to the template found in the back of the book for placement. **Trace** emblem piece to paper side (dull side) of freezer paper. **Lay** fabrics cut for each emblem section with **right sides together**. **Press** and **pin** each traced section onto corresponding fabric. **Sew** on the line **leaving raw edges open** where indicated.
Remove paper. **Trim excess** fabric leaving ¹/₈" to ¹/₄" seam allowance. **Clip** curves and points.

Turning Your Sewn Appliqué Pieces:

With wrong sides of fabric still out, **place** sewn emblem on top of the template. Make sure emblem is facing correct direction. **Cut** a slit in top layer of fabric. **Turn** and **press**.

Stitch or **press** on any small appliqué pieces indicated for your emblem.

Refer to the template for placement of any small appliqué pieces needed on your emblem and for placement in the flag.

Small Appliqué Pieces

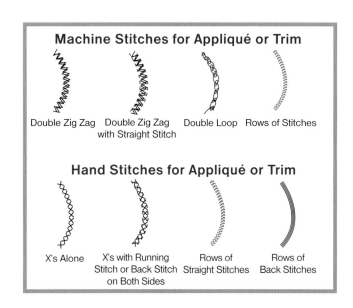

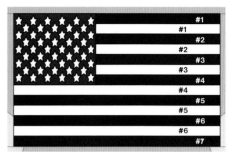

Numbered Stripes Chart

Weaving the Emblem

Position emblem piece(s) on the flag.

Follow emblem templates to center and position emblem piece(s).

Place a small gold safety pin in each seam of the flag where seam and emblem meet.

Pin emblem piece(s) in place leaving any part of the emblem below #6 red stripe loose.

Weave lower part of flag.

You will be weaving the emblem under the red stripe and over the white stripe.

Open top seam of red stripe #7 between gold pins.

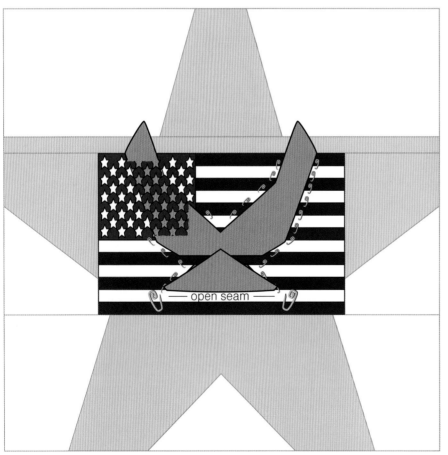

— open seam —

Pull lower portion of emblem piece through seam to the back of the quilt center.

Lay quilt out flat so seam lies in place.

Pin seam.

Using matching red thread, sew seam closed with straight stitch close to edge of red stripe.

Open bottom seam of flag between gold pins.

Bring bottom of emblem UP through seam.

Sew seam closed as before.

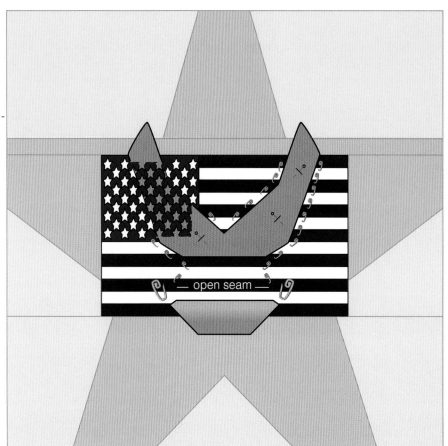

Weaving the Emblem

Remove straight pins.

Fold upper part of emblem down and open bottom seam of red stripe #6 between gold pins.

Pull emblem up through seam to back of flag.

Pin rest of emblem up to keep out of seam as you straight stitch seam closed as before.

Continue weaving the emblem into the lower portion of flag until emblem is brought up to the back of flag in the seam along the bottom of the blue star background and bottom of red stripe #4.

Use matching thread on both the blue and red fabrics as you straight stitch seam closed.

Weave under blue background of stars and upper stripes.

Open top seam of red stripe #4 between gold pins.

Open the seam of white stripe #3 and blue background of stars.

Bring emblem UP through seam to front of flag.

Weaving the Emblem

Emblems that weave under blue background:

Fold and pin emblem as shown in picture to keep emblem and stripes flat as you pin in place and sew along edge of red stripe with matching thread.

Leave seam of blue background and white stripe #3 open. You will sew this after emblem weaving is finished.

Open bottom seam of red stripe #3.

Bring emblem through to back. Topstitch seam closed as before.

Continue weaving in this manner until emblem is brought through the bottom seam of red stripe #1. Topstitch.

Open top seam of flag between gold pins.

Bring emblem up through seam to front of quilt.

Topstitch seam closed using matching blue and matching red thread.

Topstitch with matching blue thread along right side of blue background for stars to close the open seams.

Continue topstitching around blue background to make it uniform if you wish.

Finish edges of emblem.

Pin emblem edges to flag and background at open edges.

Topstitch emblem to quilt center using a stitch of your choice. See various stitches on page 7 for stitching ideas.

Place and stitch BLUE STAR with GOLD center. See page 96 for template placement.

The last step in creating your quilt is adding the borders. See page 120 for detailed instructions for adding borders to finish your quilt.

Coast Guard

yardage
Fabric requirements

Lap/Wall Size 50" x 52"

Flag and Background Star

Colors	Yardage
A – Blue	fat quarter
B – Red	1/4 yard
C – White	1/3 yard
D – Background (includes outer border)	3 yards
E – Large Star (Blue)	1 1/4 yards
F – Inner Border	1 1/3 yards

Emblem

G – Gold	2/3 yard
C2 – 2nd White	2/3 yard
A2 – 2nd Blue	fat quarter

Binding & Backing

Binding	1/2 yard
Backing	3 1/4 yards

cutting
Cut in order

Flag

	Size	Use
A – Blue	1 – 7 1/2" x 9"	Star Background
B – Red - first cut	3 strips 1 1/2" x 43"	Flag Stripes
from these cut	4 – 1 1/2" x 13"	Flag Stripes
	3 – 1 1/2" x 21 1/2"	Flag Stripes
C – White - first cut	3 strips 1 1/2" x 43"	Flag Stripes
from these cut	3 – 1 1/2" x 13"	Flag Stripes
	3 – 1 1/2" x 21 1/2"	Flag Stripes

Background Star

	Size	Use
D – Background	2 – 10 1/8" x 16 5/8"	Unit 1
	2 – 9 5/8" x 8 1/8"	Unit 2
	2 – 11 1/8" x 9 1/4"	Unit 3
	2 – 6 1/8" x 14 1/8"	Unit 3C
E – Large Star (Blue)	1 – 10 1/8" x 11 1/8"	Unit 1
	1 – 1 1/2" x 37"	Unit 1 Bottom
	2 – 10 5/8" x 8 1/8"	Unit 2
	1 – 11 1/8" x 26 3/4"	Unit 3

Inner Border

Option 1 shown here. See page 121 for yardage and cutting instructions for both options.

Outer Border (OB)

	Size	Use
D – Background	lengthwise cut	
	2 – 5" x 54"	OB Top & Bottom
	2 – 5" x 43"	OB Sides
E – Large Star (Blue)	2 – 5" x 7"	Top Star Point #1
	4 – 4" x 5"	Side Star Points #2 & #3
	4 – 6" x 7"	Bottom Star Points #4 & #5

Stars

	Star Type	Amounts
C – White	Pieced with G	1 – 1 1/2" x 14"
	Pieced with C2	1 – 1 1/2" x 14"
G – Gold	Pieced with C	1 – 1 1/2" x 14"
C2 – 2nd White	Pieced with C	1 – 1 1/2" x 14"
Solid Stars	Use remaining white and gold fabrics	

Emblem

	Size	Use
A2 - 2nd Blue	2 – 3" x 7½"	Shield Top
B - Red	6 – 1" x 4½"	Shield Stripes
C2 - 2nd White	7 – 7/8" x 4½"	Shield Stripes
	1 – 8" x 8"	Shield Back
	2 – 15" x 15"	Life Ring
G – Gold	4 – 7" x **13"**	Anchor Base
	2 – 7" x **11"**	Right Anchor Top
	2 – 6" x **6"**	Left Anchor Top

You will have circles of background to sew and appliqué for cutouts in anchor tops.
Measurements in **BOLD** should all be cut the same direction from the fabric.

Instructions given are for a Lap/Wall size quilt. If you wish to make a Queen size quilt, contact the author, Vicki Lynn Oehlke.
Phone: 701-662-6795
or email:
willowberry@gondtc.com

Coast Guard

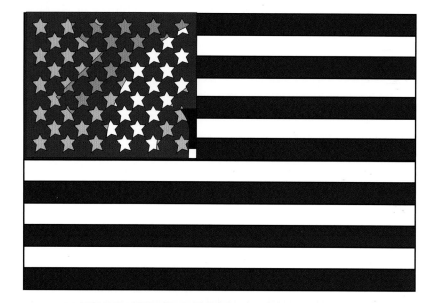

Constructing the Flag

The first step in creating your quilt is to construct the flag. This section will take you step-by-step through the process for the Coast Guard quilt.

Appliquéing the Stars

Trace 50 stars on paper side of fusible web.

Press stars to **wrong side** of fabric before cutting them out.

Refer to the "Stars Needed" chart, page 107, to find the number of star types for the Coast Guard emblem.

Templates for appliquéd stars are reversed for cutting

Star Placement Guide

For accurate star placement, refer to the full-size template found at the back of the book.

Templates for pieced stars are reversed for cutting

Stars Needed

2nd White
10

White
16

Gold
8

Pieced
14

Appliquéd Stars

	Star Number	Whole Star Base	Appliqué Over Base
	3	white	gold
	29	gold	white

Appliquéd:
2 1 gold star with C white appliqué
1 C white star with gold appliqué
Trace reversed image of star.

Preparing Pieced Stars:

Placing right sides together, **sew** the **pieced star strips**, **lengthwise** as shown, using a 1/4" seam allowance.

double pieced star strip

Right Side Up

Press seams open and **trim** seams to 1/8" or less.

Trim Seam Allowance

Refer to "Stars Needed" chart, above, and press the number of stars needed to wrong side of fabric. **Align seams** with lines on star templates.

Cut stars out on the drawn line.

Sample of Pieced Star Strips

Follow star placement guide, page 106, to arrange your stars on the blue star background.

Press stars in place.
Stitch around stars by hand or machine. See various stitches on page 7 for stitching ideas.

Preparing Appliquéd Stars:

- Use one of the fusible web stars you traced.
- Press onto the wrong side of fabric listed under "whole star base" (see chart above).
- Cut around "whole star base" on the line.

important: Be sure to leave the fusible web paper on until instructed to remove.

- Trace the shape of the "appliqué over base" star on paper side of fusible web.

- Press onto wrong side of fabric indicated in "appliqué over base" column.

- Cut out "appliqué over base" star pieces.

- Turn "whole star base" right side up. Place and press star pieces onto the "whole star base".
- Trim whole star around edges if necessary.

- Now you can remove the paper backing from the "whole star base" position and press onto the blue star background along with the other 49 stars.
- Straight stitch close to the edges of the "appliqué over base" with small stitches. Use the same colored thread as the "appliqué over base" fabric.

Piecing the Flag

note: Use a slightly longer stitch than usual as you will be ripping out large portions of these seams later. Use a regular stitch length if you don't plan to add one of the emblems.

Sew the 4 shorter red strips and 3 shorter white strips together as in diagram.

Press seams toward Red.

Sew the red & white unit to the right side of the blue background with appliquéd stars.

Press seam toward Blue.

Sew the 3 longer white strips and the 3 longer red strips together as in diagram.

Press seams toward Red.

Sew this unit to the bottom of the stars and stripes unit.

Press seam toward Red/Blue.

Flag measures:
13 1/2" x 21 1/2"

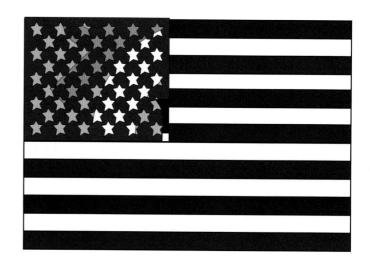

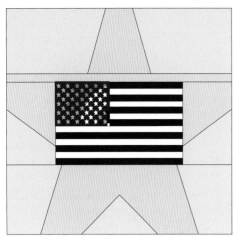

Constructing the Large Background Star

The second step in creating your quilt is to construct the large background star. This section will take you step-by-step through the process for the Coast Guard quilt.

Step 1: Preparing Background and Large Star Pieces

Measure, mark and cut from **mark to corner** as shown in diagrams with a **dotted line**.

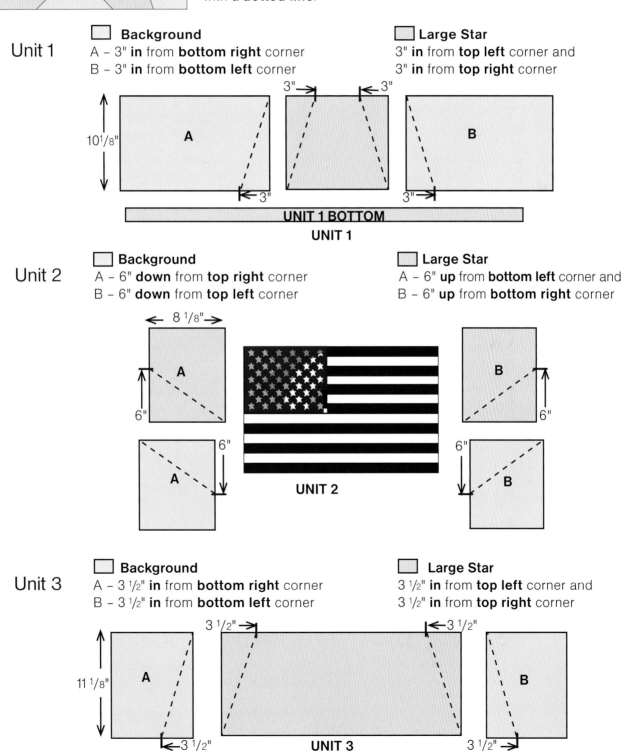

Unit 1

Background	Large Star
A – 3" in from **bottom right** corner	3" in from **top left** corner and
B – 3" in from **bottom left** corner	3" in from **top right** corner

Unit 2

Background	Large Star
A – 6" **down** from **top right** corner	A – 6" **up** from **bottom left** corner and
B – 6" **down** from **top left** corner	B – 6" **up** from **bottom right** corner

Unit 3

Background	Large Star
A – 3 1/2" **in** from **bottom right** corner	3 1/2" **in** from **top left** corner and
B – 3 1/2" **in** from **bottom left** corner	3 1/2" **in** from **top right** corner

Step 2: Pinning And Sewing

Pin And Sew Unit 1

Join Unit 1A background to **left side** of **Unit 1** large star.

Join Unit 1B background to **right side** of **Unit 1** large star.

Sew Unit 1 bottom large star blue to **bottom** of the **above joined units**.

Press toward **blue strip.**

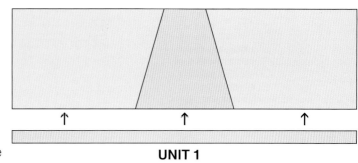

UNIT 1

Pin And Sew Unit 2

Join Unit 2A background to **Unit 2A** large star.

Join Unit 2B background to **Unit 2B** large star.

Sew Unit 2A to the **left side** of your **flag.**

Sew Unit 2B to the **right side** of your **flag.**

Press toward large star.

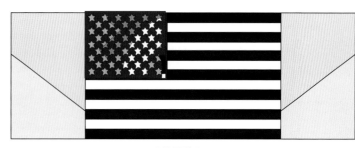

UNIT 2

Pin And Sew Unit 3

Join Unit 3A background to the **left side** of **Unit 3** large star.

Join Unit 3B background to the **right side** of **Unit 3** large star.

Press toward large star.

UNIT 3

Appliqué Unit 3C

Lay Unit 3C background star pieces **right sides together**.

Mark center of the 14 1/8" top edge.

Cut triangle
- Line up ruler from center mark to bottom right corner. Cut.
- Line up ruler from center mark to bottom left corner. Cut.

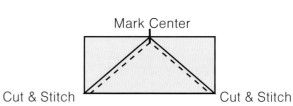

Mark Center

Cut & Stitch   Cut & Stitch

WRONG SIDE OF FABRIC

UNIT 3C

Prepare for appliqué

- Sew the two sides just cut.
- Trim top point.
- Turn right side out.
- Press.

Center appliqué

- Press pieced Unit 3 in half by lining up the two seams.
- Lay Unit 3 flat, right side up.
- Line up raw edge of triangle with the bottom edge of pieced Unit 3, and the **point** of the triangle with the pressed **crease**.
- Pin and stitch triangle to large star fabric by hand or machine.

Trim out the two layers of excess fabric from the back if you wish.

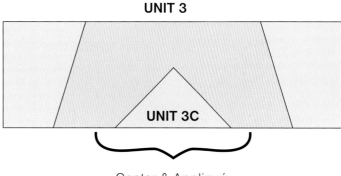

UNIT 3

UNIT 3C

Center & Appliqué

Step 3 - Joining Units

Line up the **center of the top star point** (Unit 1 – bottom edge) with the **center of the flag** (Unit 2 – top edge).

Lay flat and **pin seam** from center out.

Stitch Unit 1 to **Unit 2**.

Press seam toward the **flag**.

Line up the **flag center** (bottom edge) with the **center crease of Unit 3**.

Lay flat and **pin seam** from center out.

Stitch and **press** toward **flag**.

Trim finished quilt center if necessary.

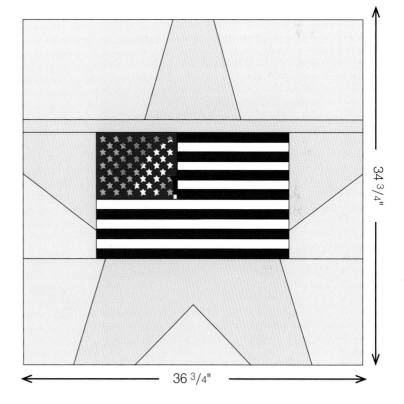

34 3/4"

36 3/4"

Adding an Emblem

The third step in creating your quilt is to add an emblem. This section will take you step-by-step through the process for the Coast Guard quilt.

note: Find the emblem templates in the back of your book.

Sewing the Emblem

Prepare Appliqué:

note: Trace the emblem from the templates located in the back of your book.

See General Instructions on page 6 for detailed description of how to prepare the appliqué.

Using the template found in the back of the book, **trace** emblem piece to paper side (dull side) of freezer paper. **Lay** fabrics cut for each emblem section with **right sides together**. **Press** and **pin** each traced section onto corresponding fabric. **Sew** on the line **leaving raw edges open** where indicated. **Remove paper**. **Trim excess** fabric leaving 1/8" to 1/4" seam allowance. **Clip** curves and points.

Turning Your Sewn Appliqué Pieces:

With wrong sides of fabric still out, **place** sewn emblem on top of the template. Make sure emblem is facing correct direction. **Cut** a slit in top layer of fabric. **Turn** and **press**.

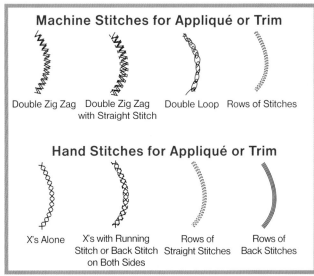

Machine Stitches for Appliqué or Trim

Double Zig Zag   Double Zig Zag with Straight Stitch   Double Loop   Rows of Stitches

Hand Stitches for Appliqué or Trim

X's Alone   X's with Running Stitch or Back Stitch on Both Sides   Rows of Straight Stitches   Rows of Back Stitches

Prepare the Shield:

Sew red and **white strips together** beginning with white and ending with white.

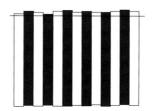

Trim one end of sewn strips to straighten, if necessary.

Sew one blue shield top rectangle to straightened edge.

Sew second blue shield top to C2 shield back.

Place pieced sections **right sides together** lining up blue fabrics.

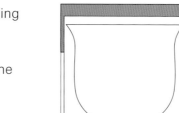

Place freezer paper shield template on top of the pieced shield back.

Center bottom point of shield in the middle of the center white stripe.

Press in place.
Stitch around shield on lines.

Remove freezer paper.

Trim seam allowance to 1/4 inch. Clip curves.

Cut slit in shield back.

The shield will be appliquéd to quilt over the flag after the main emblem has been woven and sewn in place.

Prepare Remaining Emblem Pieces:
Follow General Instructions (page 6) to prepare the following:
- Life Ring – Second White (C2)
- 2 Anchor Bottoms – Gold
- 1 Full Anchor Top Right – Gold
- 1 Partial Anchor Top Left – Gold

Holes in Anchor Tops
- Sew 2 small round appliqué pieces using Large Star Fabric.
- Appliqué one to center of each anchor top.

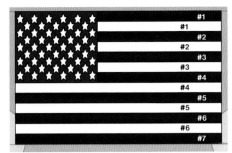

Numbered Stripes Chart

Weaving the Emblem

*Position emblem piece(s)
on the flag.*

Follow emblem templates to center
and position emblem piece(s).

Place a small gold safety pin in each
seam of the flag where seam and
emblem meet.

Pin emblem piece(s) in place leaving
any part of the emblem below #6 red
stripe loose.

Weave lower part of flag.
You will be weaving the emblem
under the red stripe and over the
white stripe.

Open top seam of red stripe #7
between gold pins.

Pull lower portion of emblem piece through seam to the back of the quilt center.

Lay quilt out flat so seam lies in place.

Pin seam.

Using matching red thread, sew seam closed with straight stitch close to edge of red stripe.

Open bottom seam of flag between gold pins.

Bring bottom of emblem up through seam.

Sew seam closed as before.

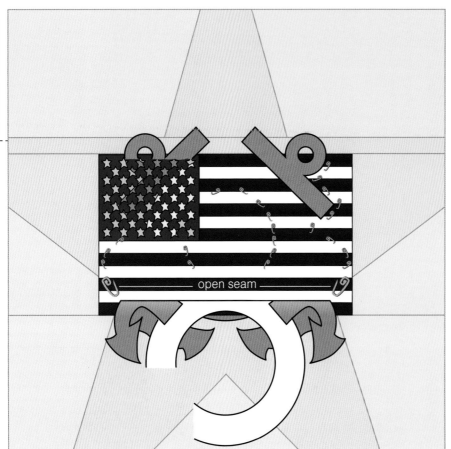

Weaving the Emblem

Remove straight pins.

Fold upper part of emblem down and open bottom seam of red stripe #6 between gold pins.

Pull emblem UP through seam to back of flag.

Pin rest of emblem up to keep out of seam as you straight stitch seam closed as before.

Continue weaving the emblem into the lower portion of flag until emblem is brought up to the back of flag in the seam along the bottom of the blue star background and bottom of red stripe #4.

Use matching thread on both the blue and red fabrics as you straight stitch seam closed.

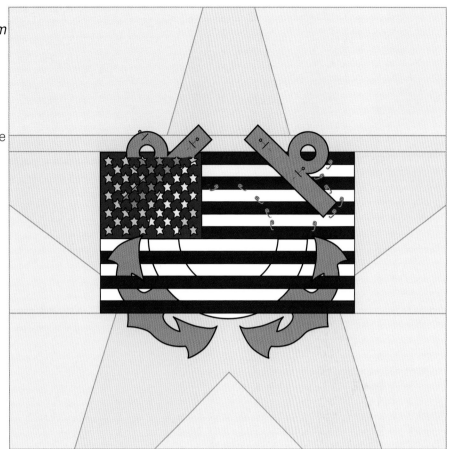

Weave under blue background of stars and upper stripes.

Open top seam of red stripe #4 between gold pins.

Bring emblem UP through seam to front of flag.

Open the seam of white stripes #1 and #2 and blue background of stars.

Weaving the Emblem

Emblems that weave under blue background:

Fold and pin emblem as shown in picture to keep emblem and stripes flat as you pin in place and sew along edge of red stripe with matching thread.

Leave seam of blue background and white stripes #1 and #2 open. You will sew this after emblem weaving is finished.

Open bottom seam of red stripe #3.

Bring emblem sections UP or DOWN through seams as needed. Topstitch seam closed as before.

Continue weaving in this manner until emblem is brought through the bottom seam of red stripe #1. Topstitch.

Open top seam of flag between gold pins.

Bring emblem sections UP or DOWN through seams as needed.

Topstitch seam closed using matching blue and matching red thread.

Topstitch with matching blue thread along right side of blue background for stars to close the open seams.

Continue topstitching around blue background to make it uniform if you wish.

Finish edges of emblem.

Pin emblem edges to flag and background at open edges.

Topstitch emblem to quilt center using a stitch of your choice. See various stitches on page 7 for stitching ideas.

Refer to template for placement of shield. Position and stitch in place.

The last step in creating your quilt is adding the borders. See page 120 for detailed instructions for adding borders to finish your quilt.

Inner Border Options

yardage

Fabric requirements

Lap/Wall Size	50" x 52"
Colors	**Yardage**
Single Fabric Inner Border	1 1/3 yards
Gold-Edged Inner Border	
G - Gold	1/3 yard
B - Black	1 1/2 yards

cutting

Inner Border	Cut	Size
Single Fabric Inner Border	lengthwise cut	4 – 4 1/2" x 45"
Gold-Edged Inner Border		
G - Gold	crosswise cut	10 – 1" x 43"
B - Black	lengthwise cut	4 – 3 1/2" x 54"

note: If you wish to **miter corners**, especially with a stripe, please follow **Option 2 – Miter Corners.**

Option 1 : SINGLE FABRIC INNER BORDER *See photo, left.*

Trim and square quilt if necessary.

Size Inner Border Strips

Measure quilt length down the center of your quilt.
Measure and trim two inner border strips to quilt length.
Pin and stitch these strips to the sides of your quilt.

Press toward inner border.
Measure quilt width including inner border sides.
Trim remaining two inner border strips to your quilt width.
Pin and stitch these strips to the top and bottom of your quilt.
Press toward inner border.

Option 2 : GOLD-EDGED INNER BORDER *See photo page 122.*

Cutting
Lap/Wall Hanging

G –Gold (Fabric Width)	10– 1" x 43"
Black (Cut lengthwise)	4 – 3 1/2" x 54"

The quilt center measures:

Approximately 33 3/4" (length) x 36 3/4" (width) for lap/wall quilt.

For the quilts in this book, it is not important that your quilt measures the above exactly. What is important is that your quilt center is square. Be sure to trim and **square** your quilt before adding the borders.

Piece Border Strips

**Piece one and one fourth – 1" strips to make eight pieces of Gold trim at least 54" long.
Sew a 54" Gold trim strip to each side of the four Black 54" strips.**

Attaching Inner Border

Center, pin, and sew a gold trimmed inner border piece to each side, top, and bottom of quilt center leaving seam 1/4" open at each end.
Press toward inner border.

Miter Corners as follows:
Place quilt right side down.

Cross loose border strips so they are laying flat.

Line up a ruler with the points shown in diagram and draw line.

Now pick up quilt, fold diagonally so the edges of the two border strips line up with right sides together.

Pin along drawn line.

Stitch from inner corner to outer edge.

Trim excess fabric.

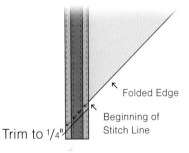

Wrong Side of Fabric

Folded Edge

Beginning of Stitch Line

Trim to 1/4"

Outer Border With Star Points

Sew the Outer Border Sides to Quilt

Measure quilt from top to bottom.
Trim Outer Border sides to same measurement.
Attach to sides of quilt.
Press toward Inner Border.

Sew the Outer Border Top and Bottom to Quilt

Measure quilt from side to side (including outer border sides).
Trim Outer Border top and bottom strips to same measurement.
Attach to top and bottom of quilt.
Press toward Inner Border.

Make Star Points

Refer to the Outer Border cutting instructions of the Service quilt you are making.
Trace Star Points onto Freezer Paper (page 124)

- One Top Star Point
- Two Side Star Points
- Two Bottom Star Points

Layer fabric pieces right sides together.
Iron traced star points to wrong side of corresponding fabric piece.
Stitch the two sides of star point leaving the bottom open.
Remove paper, trim to ¼" seam allowance.
Trim Tip of star point, turn and press.

Positioning Star Points

Lay Star Point on outer border.
Line up by placing rulers along the star edges in the quilt center.
Extend the rulers across the inner border, into the outer border.
Place Star Point in position.
You will have plenty of excess fabric in the length of your star points to allow for positioning.
Pin in place.

Sew Star Points to Quilt

Open seam and bring bottom raw edge of star point through to back of quilt.
Pin and sew seam.
Trim away excess fabric of star point.
Stitch points to outer border by hand or machine.

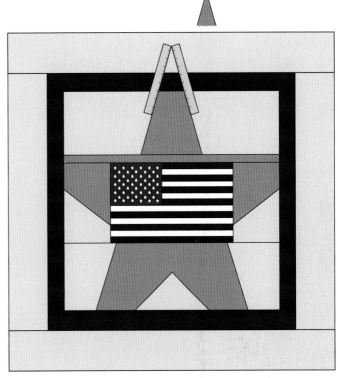

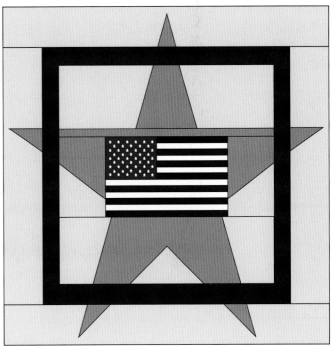

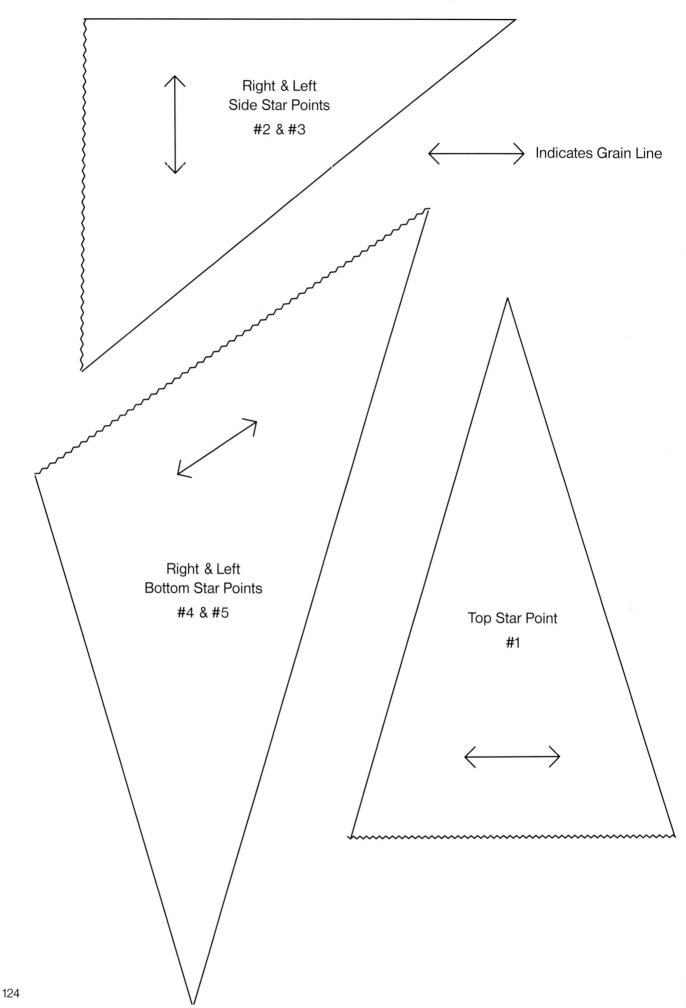

Right & Left
Side Star Points
#2 & #3

Indicates Grain Line

Right & Left
Bottom Star Points
#4 & #5

Top Star Point
#1

Label Your Quilt

The shapes on pages 126 and 127 can be used for either type of label pictured below.

Fringed Label

Sew two layers of fabric together following the outline of one of these labels.

Cut around label leaving 1/4" seam allowance.

Hand stitch to quilt back, hiding stitches in stitch line.

Fringe clipping into 1/4" seam allowance.

Brush to fray.

Label on a Background

Trace shape onto fusible web.

Iron onto wrong side of fabric.

Cut out shape. Iron onto label background.

Label Background:

Cut: 1 – 6 1/2" X 7 1/2" background
4 – 1 1/2" x 9 1/2" border strips

Stitch border strips to background.

Bind top and right edges.

Place in lower left-hand corner on back of quilt.

Sew two remaining raw edges into quilt binding.

HINTS FOR MAKING YOUR LABEL

Trace label onto paper. Use large enough sheet to allow for taping your fabric onto paper. Center your information (i.e., name & date) on the paper label.

Transfer label shape and information to fabric by taping fabric, right side up, over right side of paper label. Trace.

A light box helps tremendously.

Embroider if you wish or just use handwritten label.

Others do appreciate and thank you for labeling your quilts.

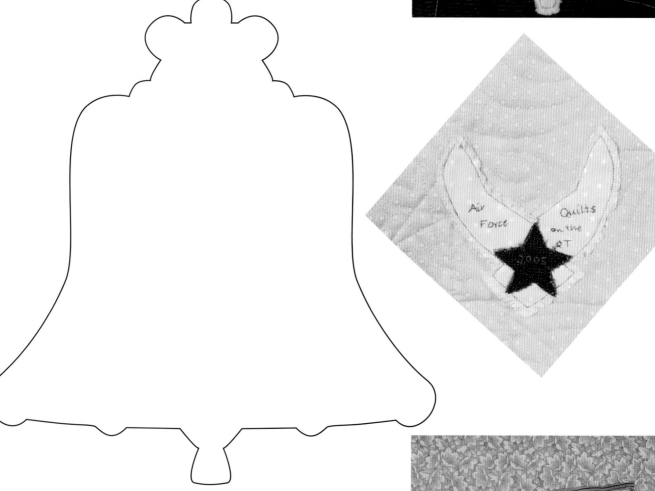

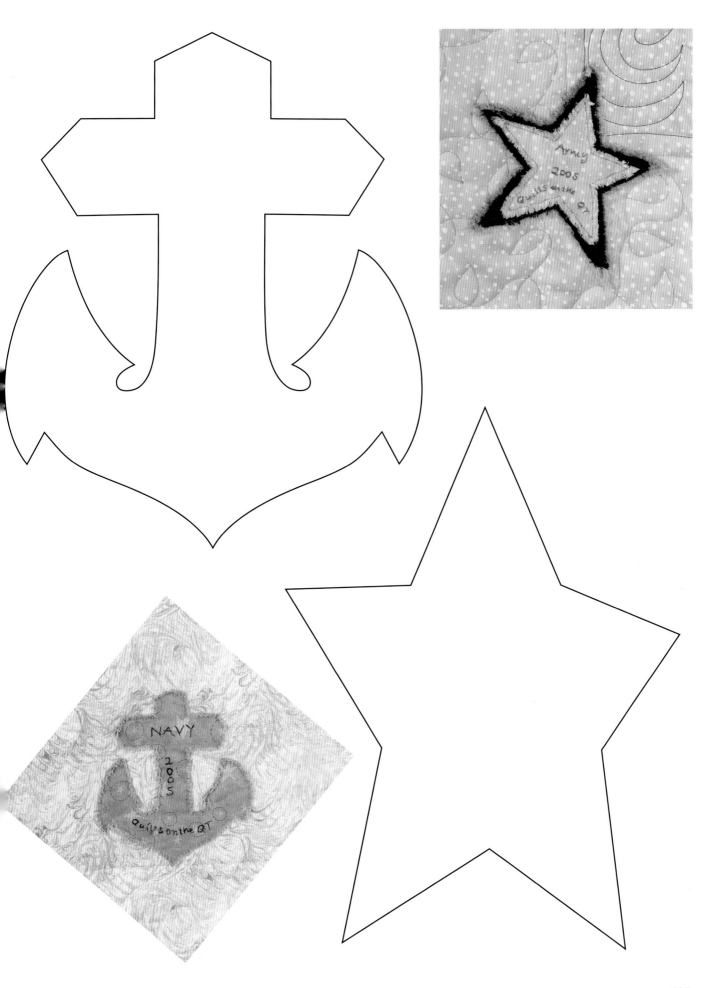

Thank yous

A heartfelt thank you to the lady soldiers of Camp Grafton.

A huge thank you to Ralph Oehlke and his wife Pearl, who showed us a wonderful time at their home along the Sheyenne River in North Dakota. Several photos were taken at Oehlkes including the one with Ralph in his original Army Uniform.

Thank you, Paul Johnson, for being our judge at the historic court room at the Old Post Office Museum in Devils Lake, North Dakota.

Photo taken at Camp Grafton Training Center "CGTC is home to the 164th Regional Training Institute, the 136th CSS Battalion and the 3662nd General Support Maintenance Company, Devils Lake, ND."

Key people who make my work so enjoyable.

Arika Johnson, *Photographer*

Joyce Hammer, *Piecing and Pattern Testing*

Laura Scott, *Graphic Artist*

Betty Jo Erickson, *Piecing and Pattern Testing*

Barb Simons, *Long Arm Machine Quilter*

Sherry Beckstrand, *Piecing and Pattern Testing*

Jeb Donavan Oehlke and Vicki Lynn

Kim Kenner, *Piecing and Pattern Testing*

OTHER HISTORICAL PHOTO LOCATIONS

Fort Abraham Lincoln *Mandan, ND*

also:
Army Quilt on wagon wheel, *p. 122*

Old Post Office Court Room *Devils Lake, ND*

also:
Justice Quilt behind jury box, *p. 24*

Ralph and Pearl Oehlke – 1881 Timber House *Kathryn, ND* *(along the Sheyenne River)*

also:
Liberty Quilt on gate, *p. 8*

Uniforms displayed with the Navy and Air Force quilts were graciously provided by:

North Dakota Maritime Museum
Dakota Bull Session
Memorial Building
Devils Lake, ND